Just Speak Up

Olga Geissler

1

Compass
Publishing

Just Speak Up 1

Olga Geissler

© 2009 Compass Publishing

Acquisitions Editor: Casey Malarcher
Content Editor: Garrett Byrne
Copy Editor: Tanya Shawlinski
Cover/Interior Design: Design Plus

Email: info@compasspub.com
http://www.compasspub.com

ISBN: 978-1-59966-416-3

19 18 17 16 15 14 13
17 16 15

Photo Credits
Unless otherwise stated, all photos are from Shutterstock Images LLC.
pp. 61, 62 © Jupiterimages
Cover © iStock International Inc.

Printed in Korea

Contents

How to Teach This Book

The best way to teach speaking is to have students practice speaking. This book has been developed to introduce a wide variety of speaking topics to students. Each unit also presents a number of activities to scaffold speaking tasks for lower-level or less secure speakers. However, it is not mandatory for higher-level and more advanced speakers to work systematically through all of the activities. Because the speaking topics are related by theme rather than specific content, the material in each unit is flexible and adaptable.

The lesson plan presented here is suggested for a class that requires significant support for each speaking task. Classes that do not require as much support may be able to jump right into the topics and start talking. It is left up to individual instructors to gauge how thoroughly each step of this lesson plan needs to be implemented in their classes.

Suggested Lesson Plan (60 min.)

Step 1

Activity 1 (10 min.)

Warm-up with Listening

Have students look at the unit topic. Ask the class to brainstorm a few possible questions they might ask someone about the topic and write them on the board. While students are suggesting possible questions, be sure to suggest the three questions that are answers for Activity 1 if students do not suggest these questions on their own (see the Answer Key for these questions). You might suggest additional questions as well for more variety.

After a reasonable list of questions is written on the board, play the audio track for Activity 1. Students will hear three speakers give short talks related to the unit topic. Based on what they hear, students should guess the question that the speaker is answering.

After playing the audio track once, replay it, but stop after each speaker. Discuss what the students heard (or did not understand), and match one of the questions on the board with the answer. Continue replaying and stopping after each speaker until all three talks have been discussed.

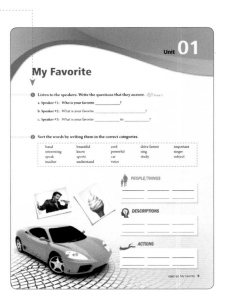

Step 2

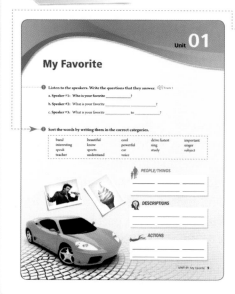

Vocabulary and Brainstorming

Have students read through the list of words and phrases as a class, focusing on their pronunciation and meaning. Then have students sort the words and phrases into the three categories provided. After everyone has finished sorting the list, check it as a class. After checking each category, ask students to brainstorm three to five additional words that could be added to the given category. All of the vocabulary brought out in this activity can help students as they answer the speaking prompts that follow in the unit.

Step 3

Model Dialogs

Play the audio track for Activity 3 and have students read along as they listen. After each dialog, stop the audio and discuss any questions student may have regarding vocabulary or grammar presented in the dialog. After all three dialogs have been heard and discussed, have students work in pairs. Pairs should practice the dialogs, taking turns saying each role.

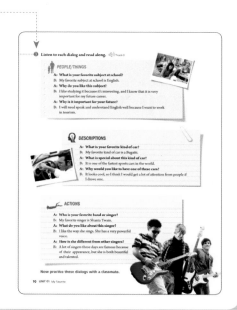

— Note

For classes that need additional pronunciation practice, replay the audio track, but stop after each line or sentence. Students should try to repeat what they hear on the audio track, focusing on their pronunciation and intonation.

Step 4

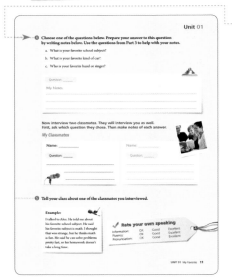

Interviews

Ask each student to choose one of the three questions to answer. Give the students a few minutes to write notes related to how they would answer the question.

Next, assign each student in the class as either "A" or "B." Have students work in A-B pairs. Have the "A" students interview "B" students. First, they should ask which question their classmate chose. "A" students may then refer back to Activity 3 to see possible questions to ask in the interview. Give students two or three minutes to collect information from their partner. Then have the "B" students interview "A" students in the same way.

When these interviews are completed, have all of the "A" students stand up and move to work with a new "B" classmate. Repeat the interview process for the new pairs.

— Note —

Because this activity is an interview, students should not feel pressure to talk at length about their answers during the interviews. Giving one or two sentences as an answer is sufficient for this activity. The interviewer should then ask a follow-up question to get more information from the interviewee until the instructor stops the interview.

Step 5

Reporting

Choose a number of students to report to the class the information they learned through one of their interviews. An example of how students can report information is provided with this activity in each unit.

As an alternative to asking only a few students to report for the class, instructors may divide the class into several groups. Then all members of each group should take turns reporting information they learned through one of their interviews. This way, all of the students in the class can participate in Activity 5.

Step 6

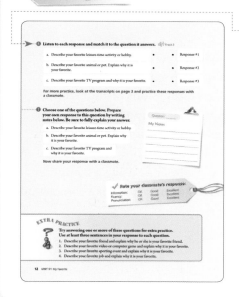

Matching and Modeling

Play the audio track for Activity 6, and have students match the given questions with one of the responses they hear. These questions and responses are meant to provide additional speaking topics and models of responses for students. While checking the answers for this activity, it may be helpful for students to read the responses shown in the transcript for the unit.

— Note —

For classes that need additional pronunciation practice, have students work in pairs reading aloud the sample responses shown in the transcript.

Step 7

Activity 7 (10 min.)

Pair Work

Have students work in pairs. One student in each pair will open his/her book. The other student will close his/her book and put it aside for the moment. The student with the open book will choose one of the questions listed in Activity 7 and write notes related to answering the question. The student who does not have a book will be the timer. The timer will look at the board while the instructor marks off increments of 10 seconds on the board. After one minute, the timer tells his/her classmate to stop making notes.

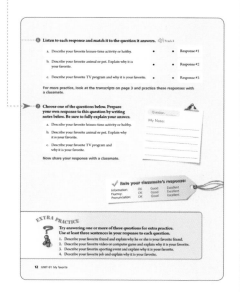

Now it is time for the student with the open book to start talking for two to three minutes (depending on the level of the class). The timer continues watching the board as the instructor marks off increments of time on the board. After the specified time, the timer tells his/her classmate to stop speaking.

The timer will now become the speaker, and the speaker will become the timer. Repeat the above process with the speaker first opening his/her book and making notes for one minute before speaking for two to three minutes.

Step 8

Extra Practice

The questions provided in the Extra Practice activity can be used in a variety of ways. Sometimes, instructors may wish to use these questions for full-class discussions of "hot" topics. Alternatively, the questions can be used for group work or pair work. The questions can also be assigned as journaling homework or speaking homework. As speaking homework, students can record their responses on a voice recorder or using a computer. These responses can be submitted to the instructor for a completion grade or for some other type of evaluation.

Note

For classes that need additional pronunciation practice, have students work in pairs reading aloud the sample responses shown in the transcript.

My Favorite

1 **Listen to the speakers. Write the questions that they answer.**  Track 1

a. **Speaker #1:** Who is your favorite _____ ?

b. **Speaker #2:** What is your favorite _____ _____ ?

c. **Speaker #3:** What is your favorite _____ to _____ ?

2 **Sort the words by writing them in the correct categories.**

band	beautiful	cool	drive	important
interesting	know	powerful	sing	singer
speak	sports car	fastest	study	subject
teacher	understand	voice		

PEOPLE/THINGS

_____ _____ _____

_____ _____ _____

DESCRIPTIONS

_____ _____ _____

_____ _____ _____

ACTIONS

_____ _____ _____

_____ _____ _____

3 Listen to each dialog and read along.  Track 2

PEOPLE/THINGS

A: **What is your favorite subject at school?**

B: My favorite subject at school is English.

A: **Why do you like this subject?**

B: I like studying it because it's interesting, and I know that it is very important for my future career.

A: **Why is it important for your future?**

B: I will need to speak and understand English well because I want to work in tourism.

DESCRIPTIONS

A: **What is your favorite kind of car?**

B: My favorite kind of car is a Bugatti.

A: **What is special about this kind of car?**

B: It is one of the fastest sports cars in the world.

A: **Why would you like to have one of these cars?**

B: It looks cool, so I think I would get a lot of attention from people if I drove one.

ACTIONS

A: **Who is your favorite band or singer?**

B: My favorite singer is Shania Twain.

A: **What do you like about this singer?**

B: I like the way she sings. She has a very powerful voice.

A: **How is she different from other singers?**

B: A lot of singers these days are famous because of their appearance, but she is both beautiful and talented.

Now practice these dialogs with a classmate.

4 Choose one of the questions below. Prepare your answer to this question by writing notes below. Use the questions from Part 3 to help with your notes.

    a. What is your favorite school subject?

    b. What is your favorite kind of car?

    c. Who is your favorite band or singer?

Question: _____

My Notes

_____

_____

_____

Now interview two classmates. They will interview you as well. First, ask which question they chose. Then make notes of each answer.

My Classmates

Name: _____

Question: _____

_____

_____

Name: _____

Question: _____

_____

_____

5 Tell your class about one of the classmates you interviewed.

Example:

I talked to Alex. He told me about his favorite school subject. He said his favorite subject is math. I thought that was strange, but he thinks math is fun. He said he can solve problems pretty fast, so his homework doesn't take a long time.

Rate your own speaking

Information:	OK	Good	Excellent
Fluency:	OK	Good	Excellent
Pronunciation:	OK	Good	Excellent

6 Listen to each response and match it to the question it answers. 🔊 Track 3

a. Describe your favorite leisure-time activity or hobby.   •   • Response #1

b. Describe your favorite animal or pet. Explain why it is your favorite.   •   • Response #2

c. Describe your favorite TV program and why it is your favorite.   •   • Response #3

For more practice, look at the transcripts on page 1 and practice these responses with a classmate.

7 **Choose one of the questions below. Prepare your own response to this question by writing notes in the provided space. Be sure to explain your answer.**

a. Describe your favorite leisure-time activity or hobby.

b. Describe your favorite animal or pet. Explain why it is your favorite.

c. Describe your favorite TV program and why it is your favorite.

Now share your response with a classmate.

Question: _____

My Notes

_____
_____
_____
_____
_____

Rate your classmate's response:

	OK	Good	Excellent
Information:	OK	Good	Excellent
Fluency:	OK	Good	Excellent
Pronunciation:	OK	Good	Excellent

EXTRA PRACTICE

Try answering one or more of these questions for extra practice. Use at least three sentences in your response to each question.

1. Describe your favorite friend and explain why he or she is your favorite friend.
2. Describe your favorite video or computer game and explain why it is your favorite.
3. Describe your favorite sporting event and explain why it is your favorite.
4. Describe your favorite job and explain why it is your favorite.

My Country

---

① **Listen to the speakers. Write the questions that they answer.** 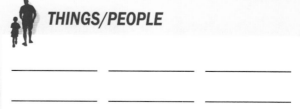 Track 4

a. Speaker #1: What is a _____ _____ from your country?

b. Speaker #2: What is a _____ _____ in your country?

c. Speaker #3: What are _____ _____ in your country?

---

② **Sort the words by writing them in the correct categories.**

architecture	capital	foreigner	grow	hear
hold on to	immigrate	large	less than	live
native	official	population	size	speak
territory	the same as	well known		

ACTIONS

_____ _____ _____

_____ _____ _____

THINGS/PEOPLE

_____ _____ _____

_____ _____ _____

DESCRIPTIONS

_____ _____ _____

_____ _____ _____

3 Listen to each dialog and read along. Track 5

ACTIONS

A: **How big is your native country?**

B: The territory of my native country isn't very large. It is probably the same size as Germany.

A: **How many people live there?**

B: There are less than five million people in my country.

A: **Is the population growing very fast?**

B: Not really. But I think a lot of foreigners have started immigrating to my country in recent years.

THINGS/PEOPLE

A: **What are the official languages of your native country?**

B: There are two official languages in my country. They are Irish and English.

A: **Which of those languages is spoken by more people?**

B: English is spoken throughout the country, but in some parts, people speak Irish.

A: **Do any people speak other languages as well?**

B: You might hear people speaking Polish and Chinese. There are lots of people from Poland and China in my country.

DESCRIPTIONS

A: **What is the capital city of your country?**

B: The capital city of my country is Rome.

A: **What is it like?**

B: Rome is a very old but very beautiful city. It is located in the western part of the country.

A: **Is it known for anything?**

B: Rome is well known for its architecture and the fact that it has held on to many old traditions.

Now practice these dialogs with a classmate.

4 **Choose one of the questions below. Prepare your answer to this question by writing notes below. Use the questions from Part 3 to help with your notes.**

   a. How big is your native country? How many people live there?

   b. What are the official languages of your native country?

   c. What is the capital city of your country? Is this city known for anything?

Question: _____

My Notes

_____

_____

_____

Now interview two classmates. They will interview you as well. First, ask which question they chose. Then make notes of each answer.

My Classmates

Name: _____

Question: _____ -

_____

_____

_____

Name: _____

Question: _____

_____

_____

_____

5 **Tell your class about one of the classmates you interviewed.**

Example:

I talked to Betty. She explained that the official language in Japan is Japanese. Everybody learns Japanese in school. Betty said that they also teach some Chinese and English in schools. But Japanese is the only official language.

✔ **Rate your own speaking**

Information:	OK	Good	Excellent
Fluency:	OK	Good	Excellent
Pronunciation:	OK	Good	Excellent

6 Listen to each response and match it to the question it answers. ◄))) Track 6

    a. What are the main universities and colleges in your country?   ●   ●   Response #1

    b. What are the best restaurants in your native country?   ●   ●   Response #2

    c. Which theme parks in your country are the most popular?   ●   ●   Response #3

For more practice, look at the transcripts on page 1 and practice these responses with a classmate.

7 **Choose one of the questions below. Prepare your own response to this question by writing notes in the provided space. Be sure to explain your answer.**

Question: _____

My Notes

    a. What are the main universities and colleges in your country?

    b. What are the best restaurants in your native country?

    c. Which theme parks in your country are the most popular?

Now share your response with a classmate.

✔ Rate your classmate's response:

Information:	OK	Good	Excellent
Fluency:	OK	Good	Excellent
Pronunciation:	OK	Good	Excellent

 EXTRA PRACTICE

Try answering one or more of these questions for extra practice. Use at least three sentences in your response to each question.

1. Describe the culture and traditions in your native country.
2. What are the traditional clothes in your native country?
3. Where can people see performances or enjoy the circus in your native country?
4. What are the most popular vacation destinations in your country?

Studying English

1 **Listen to the speakers. Write the questions that they answer.** 🔊 Track 7

a. Speaker #1: What is a good thing to _____ _____ _____ ?

b. Speaker #2: Why is it important to _____ _____ _____?

c. Speaker #3: How did you learn to _____ _____?

2 **Sort the words by writing them in the correct categories.**

definition	focus on	friends	grammar	improve
master	native speakers	others	parents	practice
pronounce	sentences	songs	straight As	students
teachers	tenses	watch		

ACTIONS

_____ _____ _____

_____ _____ _____

PEOPLE

_____ _____ _____

_____ _____ _____

THINGS

_____ _____ _____

_____ _____ _____

3 **Listen to each dialog and read along.** Track 8

ACTIONS

A: Do you think it is important to study English grammar?

B: Yes, studying English grammar is very important for mastering English.

A: What should you focus on?

B: You should especially focus on studying tenses.

A: Why is it important to focus on this?

B: This way, you can learn to form more sentences in different tenses.

 ### PEOPLE

A: What do you think the best ways to practice speaking English are?

B: There are a lot of ways to practice speaking English. First, you should find every chance to speak English.

A: Who can you practice speaking with?

B: You can practice speaking with your friends, teachers, or native speakers.

A: What else should you do?

B: You should also watch English TV and listen to English songs. That can help you learn how to pronounce words correctly.

DESCRIPTIONS

A: What is your definition of a "good student?"

B: My definition of a good student is a student who tries hard.

A: Does that mean a good student always gets straight As?

B: In my opinion, a good student is not necessarily a straight A student.

A: How can you tell if a student fits your definition?

B: As long as others, like parents and teachers, can see that the student is trying hard to improve, then that student fits my definition of a "good student."

Now practice these dialogs with a classmate.

4 **Choose one of the questions below. Prepare your answer to this question by writing notes below. Use the questions from Part 3 to help with your notes.**

a. Do you think it is important to study English grammar?

b. What do you think the best ways to practice speaking English?

c. What is your definition of a "good student?"

Question: _____

My Notes

_____

_____

_____

Now interview two classmates. They will interview you as well. First, ask which question they chose. Then make notes of each answer.

My Classmates

Name: _____

Question: _____

_____

_____

_____

Name: _____

Question: _____

_____

_____

_____

5 **Tell your class about one of the classmates you interviewed.**

Example:

I talked to Carl. He told me how he uses TV shows and English songs to help him learn English. He said he uses both for listening practice. He doesn't always understand everything, but he still enjoys watching TV and listening to music. He said he sometimes tries to sing English songs to work on his pronunciation.

✔ **Rate your own speaking**

Information:	OK	Good	Excellent
Fluency:	OK	Good	Excellent
Pronunciation:	OK	Good	Excellent

6 Listen to each response and match it to the question it answers. 🔊 Track 9

a. How can you learn to read at a fast pace? Explain.   •   • Response #1

b. What are the best strategies for learning new vocabulary?   •   • Response #2

c. How can watching TV and listening to songs in English help with your English language studies?   •   • Response #3

For more practice, look at the transcripts on page 2 and practice these responses with a classmate.

7 Choose one of the questions below. Prepare your own response to this question by writing notes in the provided space. Be sure to explain your answer.

Question: _____

My Notes

_____
_____
_____
_____
_____

a. How can you learn to read at a fast pace? Explain.

b. What are the best strategies for learning new vocabulary?

c. How can watching TV and listening to songs in English help with your English language studies?

Now share your response with a classmate.

✔ Rate your classmate's response:

Information:	OK	Good	Excellent
Fluency:	OK	Good	Excellent
Pronunciation:	OK	Good	Excellent

 EXTRA PRACTICE

Try answering one or more of these questions for extra practice. Use at least three sentences in your response to each question.

1. Why is it important to be on time for class?
2. What should you do and not do in class?
3. Why is it important to do your homework regularly?
4. How did you learn to read English? Do you think it was easy or difficult?

Movies

1 **Listen to the speakers. Write the questions that they answer.**  Track 10

a. Speaker #1: Who is your _____ _____?

b. Speaker #2: Do you like _____ _____?

c. Speaker #3: What is an _____ _____?

2 **Sort the words by writing them in the correct categories.**

always	cheaper	drive-in	expensive	fun
membership card	months before	never	new	often
price	rainy	screen	sound system	tickets
usually	every weekend	wide		

THINGS

_____ _____ _____

_____ _____ _____

TIMES

_____ _____ _____

_____ _____ _____

DESCRIPTIONS

_____ _____ _____

_____ _____ _____

3 **Listen to each dialog and read along.** Track 11

🕐 TIMES

A: **Do you like going to the movies? Explain.**

B: Yes, I really enjoy going to see new movies.

A: **Who do you usually go to movies with?**

B: I usually go with my friends every other weekend.

A: **Do you spend a lot of money going to the movies?**

B: Not really. We have membership cards, so we always get tickets for the movies at a cheaper price.

📦 THINGS

A: **What are the advantages of watching a movie in a movie theater?**

B: The advantages are the wide screen and the sound system that is used.

A: **Can you think of any additional advantages?**

B: Also, you usually see movies in a movie theater months before they come out on TV.

A: **Can you think of any disadvantages of watching a movie in a movie theater?**

B: One disadvantage is that it is expensive. Also, sometimes people make noise and ruin the movie.

💡 DESCRIPTIONS

A: **Are drive-in movie theaters popular in your country?**

B: No, I don't actually think there are any drive-in movie theaters in my country.

A: **Why do you think this is the case?**

B: This is probably because the weather is not very nice. It's rainy and cold outdoors quite often.

A: **Have you ever watched a movie at a drive-in movie theater?**

B: No, I've never been to a drive-in movie theater. I don't think it would be fun to see a movie there, anyway.

Now practice these dialogs with a classmate.

4 **Choose one of the questions below. Prepare your answer to this question by writing notes below. Use the questions from Part 3 to help with your notes.**

a. Do you like going to the movies? Explain.

b. What are the advantages and disadvantages of watching a movie in a movie theater?

c. Are drive-in movie theaters popular in your country?

Question: _____

My Notes

_____

_____

_____

Now interview two classmates. They will interview you as well. First, ask which question they chose. Then make notes of each answer.

My Classmates

Name: _____

Question: _____

_____

_____

_____

Name: _____

Question: _____

_____

_____

_____

5 **Tell your class about one of the classmates you interviewed.**

Example:

I talked to Donna. She told me why she likes going to movies. She said that she likes to go to movies because they are relaxing for her. She usually watches comedies or sometimes romantic movies. Donna said she would go to the movies every day if she could.

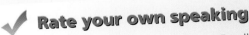

✔ **Rate your own speaking**

Information:	OK	Good	Excellent
Fluency:	OK	Good	Excellent
Pronunciation:	OK	Good	Excellent

6 Listen to each response and match it to the question it answers. 🔊 Track 12

    a. Do you pay attention to movie ratings when you choose a movie to watch? Why or why not?

    •   •   Response #1

    b. Should children be allowed to watch horror movies? Explain.

    •   •   Response #2

    c. Where is the center of your national movie industry located?

    •   •   Response #3

For more practice, look at the transcripts on page 2 and practice these responses with a classmate.

7 **Choose one of the questions below. Prepare your own response to this question by writing notes in the provided space. Be sure to explain your answer.**

    a. Do you pay attention to movie ratings when you choose a movie to watch? Why or why not?

    b. Should children be allowed to watch horror movies? Explain.

    c. Where is the center of your national movie industry located?

Now share your response with a classmate.

Question: _____

My Notes

_____
_____
_____
_____
_____

✔ Rate your classmate's response:

Information:	OK	Good	Excellent
Fluency:	OK	Good	Excellent
Pronunciation:	OK	Good	Excellent

EXTRA PRACTICE

Try answering one or more of these questions for extra practice. Use at least three sentences in your response to each question.

    1. Who is your favorite actor/actress? Why?
    2. Why do some people like watching horror movies?
    3. Do you think animated movies are only for children? Explain.
    4. What is an action movie? Give examples of famous action movies in your country.

Restaurants

1 **Listen to the speakers. Write the questions that they answer.** 🔊 Track 13

a. Speaker #1: What was the _____ _____ you went to?

b. Speaker #2: What _____ do you usually order when you eat out?

c. Speaker #3: Why is _____ good for your health?

2 **Sort the words by writing them in the correct categories.**

appetizer	cook	different	healthier	homemade
main course	meal	noodle	opportunity	order
particular	prefer	prepare	sample	spring rolls
traditional	travel	various		

THINGS

_____ _____ _____

_____ _____ _____

ACTIONS

_____ _____ _____

_____ _____ _____

DESCRIPTIONS

_____ _____ _____

_____ _____ _____

3 **Listen to each dialog and read along.** Track 14

THINGS

A: **Do you prefer to eat out or to eat at home?**

B: Maybe I am too traditional, but I prefer to eat at home.

A: **What do you prefer about eating there?**

B: I enjoy the company of my family and the quality time we have together.

A: **Can you think of a particularly good point about your preference?**

B: I like it when we prepare our homemade food and eat it together.
I'm sure the meals are healthier that way.

ACTIONS

A: **When you eat out, do you like to order appetizers?**

B: Yes, I like to order different kinds of appetizers when I eat out. I like to sample various things before I have my main course.

A: **What appetizers do you order when you eat out?**

B: It depends on the kind of restaurant I go to, but I usually have spring rolls.

A: **Where is a good restaurant for this appetizer?**

B: A good restaurant for spring rolls is the Vietnamese noodle house near my apartment.

DESCRIPTIONS

A: **Is it a good idea to eat out when you travel to other countries?**

B: Of course! I think people should use the opportunity to sample food from different countries when they travel abroad.

A: **Why?**

B: Because it is one way to learn about various cultures in other countries.

A: **Are there any other reasons?**

B: Another good reason for eating out when you travel is so that you don't have to cook. Who wants to cook when they're on vacation? Not me!

Now practice these dialogs with a classmate.

4 **Choose one of the questions below. Prepare your answer to this question by writing notes below. Use the questions from Part 3 to help with your notes.**

a. Do you prefer to eat out or to eat at home? Explain.

b. When you eat out, do you like to order appetizers? If so, what?

c. Is it a good idea to eat out when you travel to other countries? Explain.

Question: _____

My Notes

_____

_____

_____

**Now interview two classmates. They will interview you as well.
First, ask which question they chose. Then make notes of each answer.**

My Classmates

Name: _____

Question: _____

_____

_____

_____

Name: _____

Question: _____

_____

_____

_____

5 **Tell your class about one of the classmates you interviewed.**

Example:

I talked to Ed. He told me about the kinds of appetizers he likes to order in restaurants. His favorite appetizer is fried calamari. That's fried squid, in case you didn't know. He said that in his country, squid is very popular. He grew up eating it, so he really likes it.

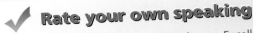

✔ **Rate your own speaking**

Information:	OK	Good	Excellent
Fluency:	OK	Good	Excellent
Pronunciation:	OK	Good	Excellent

6 Listen to each response and match it to the question it answers. 🔊 Track 15

    a. What is your favorite restaurant?

    •   • Response #1

    b. What types of dessert do you like to order?

    •   • Response #2

    c. When you go out, do you try different restaurants, or do you usually go to the same one?

    •   • Response #3

For more practice, look at the transcripts on page 3 and practice these responses with a classmate.

7 Choose one of the questions below. Prepare your own response to this question by writing notes in the provided space. Be sure to explain your answer.

    a. What is your favorite restaurant?

    b. What types of dessert do you like to order?

    c. When you go out, do you try different restaurants, or do you usually go to the same one?

Now share your response with a classmate.

Question: _____

My Notes

_____
_____
_____
_____
_____

✓ Rate your classmate's response:

	OK	Good	Excellent
Information:	OK	Good	Excellent
Fluency:	OK	Good	Excellent
Pronunciation:	OK	Good	Excellent

Try answering one or more of these questions for extra practice. Use at least three sentences in your response to each question.

1. What is a traditional food in your culture? How is it prepared?
2. When you go to your favorite restaurant, what do you usually order? Why?
3. Do you like to eat at fast-food restaurants? Why or why not?
4. Describe a bad experience that you had in a restaurant.

Music

① **Listen to the speakers. Write the questions that they answer.** 🔊 Track 16

a. **Speaker #1:** What is your favorite _____ _____?

b. **Speaker #2:** Do you like to _____ _____ _____?

c. **Speaker #3:** When was the last time you _____ _____ _____?

② **Sort the words by writing them in the correct categories.**

annoying	classical music	club	dance music	distracting
energetic	heavy metal	jazz	Latin pop	loud
piano	rap music	saxophone	school	situation
sound	wonderful	young		

KINDS OF MUSIC

_____ _____

_____ _____

DESCRIPTIONS

_____ _____ _____

_____ _____ _____

THINGS

_____ _____ _____

_____ _____ _____

3 **Listen to each dialog and read along.** 🔊 Track 17

🎵 KINDS OF MUSIC

A: **What is your favorite kind of music?**

B: My favorite kind of music is Latin pop because it is the music that I grew up with.

A: **Where can you hear this music?**

B: Latin pop is mostly used as dance music, so it is played in dance clubs.

A: **What do you like about this music?**

B: It is energetic, so it makes me want to dance. I really like dancing.

💡 DESCRIPTIONS

A: **Do you play any musical instruments?**

B: Yes, I do. I play the piano. I like playing classical music on the piano.

A: **How long have you played this instrument?**

B: My parents took me to a music school when I was very young. I guess I was about seven when I started learning to play the piano.

A: **Are there any other instruments you would like to learn to play?**

B: I would love to learn to play the saxophone because I think it has a wonderful sound.

📦 THINGS

A: **Describe a situation when music can be distracting.**

B: Music can be distracting when it is too loud. Loud rap music or heavy metal can be very annoying.

A: **Is it distracting even if it is your favorite kind of music?**

B: Yes, when somebody is playing jazz, my favorite kind of music, too loud, I still wouldn't enjoy it. It would bother me.

A: **When else can music be distracting?**

B: Music can also be very distracting when you are doing homework.

Now practice these dialogs with a classmate.

4 **Choose one of the questions below. Prepare your answer to this question by writing notes below. Use the questions from Part 3 to help with your notes.**

a. What is your favorite kind of music? What do you like about it?

b. Do you play any musical instruments? If so, how long have you been playing?

c. Describe a situation when music can be distracting.

Question: _____

My Notes

_____

_____

_____

Now interview two classmates. They will interview you as well. First, ask which question they chose. Then make notes of each answer.

My Classmates

Name: _____

Question: _____

_____

_____

_____

Name: _____

Question: _____

_____

_____

_____

5 **Tell your class about one of the classmates you interviewed.**

Example:

I talked to Fran. She told me about a situation when music can be distracting. She said that when she studies, music is distracting for her. It has to be completely quiet when she studies, so she likes studying in the library. People can only listen to music on their MP3 players there, so she doesn't get distracted.

✔ **Rate your own speaking**

Information:	OK	Good	Excellent
Fluency:	OK	Good	Excellent
Pronunciation:	OK	Good	Excellent

6 **Listen to each response and match it to the question it answers.** Track 18

    a. Are you a good singer? Explain.   ●   ● Response #1

    b. How can music help you to learn English?   ●   ● Response #2

    c. When was the last time you went to a concert?   ●   ● Response #3

For more practice, look at the transcripts on page 3 and practice these responses with a classmate.

7 **Choose one of the questions below. Prepare your own response to this question by writing notes in the provided space. Be sure to explain your answer.**

    a. Are you a good singer? Explain.

    b. How can music help you to learn English?

    c. When was the last time you went to a concert?

Now share your response with a classmate.

Question: _____

My Notes

_____

_____

_____

_____

_____

Rate your classmate's response:

Information:	OK	Good	Excellent
Fluency:	OK	Good	Excellent
Pronunciation:	OK	Good	Excellent

EXTRA PRACTICE

Try answering one or more of these questions for extra practice. Use at least three sentences in your response to each question.

1. Describe how music can influence your mood.
2. How is your taste in music different from your parents'? Give examples.
3. What is your favorite style of dancing? Are you good at it? Explain.
4. What is your favorite radio station? When do you listen to it?

Name Them

1 **Listen to the speakers. Write the questions that they answer.** (((•))) Track 19

a. Speaker #1: Who are some _____ _____?

b. Speaker #2: What are some _____ _____?

c. Speaker #3: What are some _____ _____?

2 **Sort the words by writing them in the correct categories.**

China	ending	heaven	India	tell
meter	Paris	read	recommend	record
sights	100 meter sprint	talk about	Los Angeles	tower
visit	win	Windsor Palace		

THINGS

_____ _____ _____

_____ _____ _____

PLACES

_____ _____ _____

_____ _____ _____

ACTIONS

_____ _____ _____

_____ _____ _____

3 **Listen to each dialog and read along.** (((•))) Track 20

 THINGS

A: **What are the titles of some famous books?**

B: Some famous books that I know are *The Alchemist*, *The Five People You Meet in Heaven*, and *Life of Pi*.

A: **Have you read any of these books?**

B: Yes, I read *Life of Pi*. It is a very interesting book about a boy from India and a tiger.

A: **Would you recommend this book?**

B: It has a very good ending. I would highly recommend this book.

PLACES

A: **What are some famous cities in the world?**

B: The most famous cities in the world are Los Angeles, New York, London, Paris, and Tokyo.

A: **Tell me something about one of these cities.**

B: I visited London once. It is best known for sights like Big Ben, Windsor Palace, and the Tower of London.

A: **How big is this city?**

B: Maybe about 14 million people live there.

PEOPLE

A: **Who are some famous athletes?**

B: Some famous athletes these days are Michael Phelps, Usain Bolt, and Kelly Holmes.

A: **Tell me something about one of these athletes.**

B: Usain Bolt is famous because he won the Olympics in China. He set a new world record for the 100-meter sprint.

A: **Is there anything unique or unusual about this athlete?**

B: He is kind of unusual because he is so tall and sprinters are not usually that tall.

Now practice these dialogs with a classmate.

4 **Choose one of the questions below. Prepare your answer to this question by writing notes below. Use the questions from Part 3 to help with your notes.**

a. What are the titles of some famous books? Have you read any of these books?

b. What are some famous cities in the world? Describe one of them.

c. Who are some famous athletes? Describe one of them.

Question: _____

My Notes

_____

_____

_____

Now interview two classmates. They will interview you as well. First, ask which question they chose. Then make notes of each answer.

My Classmates

Name: _____

Question: _____

_____

_____

_____

Name: _____

Question: _____

_____

_____

5 **Tell your class about one of the classmates you interviewed.**

Example:

I talked to Greg. He told me about the titles of some famous books. Three books that he thought of are *Moby Dick, Huckleberry Finn,* and *The Odyssey.* He said he read all three of those books. He didn't read them in English, of course. He read them in his native language.

✔ **Rate your own speaking**

Information:	OK	Good	Excellent
Fluency:	OK	Good	Excellent
Pronunciation:	OK	Good	Excellent

6 Listen to each response and match it to the question it answers. (◁))) Track 21

    a. Give the names of three famous actresses and talk about one of them.

    •   • Response #1

    b. Give the titles of three famous songs and talk about one of them.

    •   • Response #2

    c. Give the names of three famous writers and talk about one of them.

    •   • Response #3

For more practice, look at the transcripts on page 4 and practice these responses with a classmate.

7 **Choose one of the questions below. Prepare your own response to this question by writing notes in the provided space. Be sure to explain your answer.**

    a. Give the names of three famous actresses and talk about one of them.

    b. Give the titles of three famous songs and talk about one of them.

    c. Give the names of three famous writers and talk about one of them.

Now share your response with a classmate.

Question: _____

My Notes

_____
_____
_____
_____
_____

✔ **Rate your classmate's response:**

Information:	OK	Good	Excellent
Fluency:	OK	Good	Excellent
Pronunciation:	OK	Good	Excellent

EXTRA PRACTICE

Try answering one or more of these questions for extra practice. Use at least three sentences in your response to each question.

    1. Give the names of three famous actors and talk about one of them.
    2. Give the names of three famous singers and talk about one of them.
    3. Give the titles of three famous movies and talk about one of them.
    4. Give the titles of three famous TV shows and talk about one of them.

The Environment

1 **Listen to the speakers. Write the questions that they answer.**  Track 22

a. **Speaker #1:** What is one way to _____ _____?

b. **Speaker #2:** What is an effect of _____ _____?

c. **Speaker #3:** What is _____ _____?

2 **Sort the words by writing them in the correct categories.**

plants	grow	glass	drink	land
paper	recycle	streams	collect	cloth
produce	cardboard	plastic	metal	trees
rivers	animals	pollute		

NATURE

_____ _____ _____

_____ _____ _____

ACTIONS

_____ _____ _____

_____ _____ _____

MATERIALS

_____ _____ _____

_____ _____ _____

3 **Listen to each dialog and read along.** Track 23

 NATURE

A: **Why is it bad for the environment when cities grow and take up more land?**

B: It is harmful for the environment because there is less land available for trees and other plants to grow and for animals to live.

A: **What happens when there are fewer plants?**

B: Plants produce oxygen. Fewer plants mean less oxygen is produced.

A: **Why is oxygen important?**

B: Living things need oxygen to survive.

ACTIONS

A: **What are the effects of polluting water? Explain.**

B: Our water comes from rivers and streams. The main danger of polluting this water is that people have to use or drink it.

A: **What happens if the water in rivers or streams is polluted?**

B: If this happens, the amount of available clean, fresh water will not be enough for everyone to drink.

A: **Why is fresh water important?**

B: People and animals cannot drink salt water. Plants need fresh water, too.

 MATERIALS

A: **What household items can be recycled?**

B: We can recycle paper, cardboard, cloth, plastic, metal, and glass.

A: **What do you collect at home for recycling?**

B: My family and I collect old newspapers, magazines, old clothes, milk cartons, plastic containers, and aluminum cans to be recycled.

A: **Why is recycling important?**

B: Recycling is important because it means that we can reuse a lot of things. This conserves resources.

Now practice these dialogs with a classmate.

4 **Choose one of the questions below. Prepare your answer to this question by writing notes below. Use the questions from Part 3 to help with your notes.**

a. Why is it dangerous for the environment when cities grow and take up more land?

b. What are the effects of polluting water? Explain.

c. What household items can be recycled? What do you collect at home for recycling?

Question: _____

My Notes

_____

_____

_____

Now interview two classmates. They will interview you as well. First, ask which question they chose. Then make notes of each answer.

My Classmates

Name: _____

Question: _____

_____

_____

_____

Name: _____

Question: _____

_____

_____

_____

5 **Tell your class about one of the classmates you interviewed.**

Example:

I talked to Helga. She explained some of the effects of polluting water. The first effect she talked about was how pollution kills fish. She also mentioned that water with a lot of pollution in it can also kill people if they drink it. Naturally, she said it's bad to pollute water that is used by people.

Rate your own speaking

Information:	OK	Good	Excellent
Fluency:	OK	Good	Excellent
Pronunciation:	OK	Good	Excellent

6 Listen to each response and match it to the question it answers. Track 24

    a. Is there a lot of traffic in your city? What do you think people should do to reduce traffic?

    b. What can people do at home to save water?

    c. How does cutting down trees affect the environment?

    • Response #1

    • Response #2

    • Response #3

For more practice, look at the transcripts on page 4 and practice these responses with a classmate.

7 **Choose one of the questions below. Prepare your own response to this question by writing notes in the provided space. Be sure to explain your answer.**

    a. Is there a lot of traffic in your city? What do you think people should do to reduce traffic?

    b. What can people do at home to save water?

    c. How does cutting down trees affect the environment?

Now share your response with a classmate.

Question: _____

My Notes

_____

_____

_____

_____

_____

Rate your classmate's response:

	OK	Good	Excellent
Information:	OK	Good	Excellent
Fluency:	OK	Good	Excellent
Pronunciation:	OK	Good	Excellent

EXTRA PRACTICE

Try answering one or more of these questions for extra practice. Use at least three sentences in your response to each question.

1. Why is it important to use electricity wisely? Explain.
2. What national parks and nature reserves do you have in your country?
3. Why is it important for people to clean up garbage in picnic areas before they leave?
4. What can children do to help preserve the environment?

Everyday Activities

1 **Listen to the speakers. Write the questions that they answer.** 🔊 Track 25

    a. Speaker #1: What time do you _____ _____?

    b. Speaker #2: What do you do _____ _____?

    c. Speaker #3: What do you do on _____ _____ _____?

2 **Sort the words by writing them in the correct categories.**

breakfast	cookie	eat	evening	relax
pizza	dinner	morning	oatmeal	watch
leave	bread	cook	noon	pancakes
salad	lunch	show		

🍴 **MEALS/MEALTIMES**

_____ _____ _____

_____ _____ _____

🌭 **FOOD**

_____ _____ _____

_____ _____ _____

ACTIONS

_____ _____ _____

_____ _____ _____

3 **Listen to each dialog and read along.**  Track 26

 MEALS/MEALTIMES

A: What time do you usually have breakfast?

B: I usually have my breakfast at around seven o'clock in the morning.

A: Who prepares your breakfast?

B: My mom usually cooks it for me, but when she has to go to work early, I make breakfast myself.

A: What do you have for breakfast?

B: I usually have bread or oatmeal. On weekends, I have pancakes!

FOOD

A: What time do you usually have lunch?

B: I usually have lunch at around noon. Because I have breakfast at seven, I am usually very hungry by then.

A: Where do you usually eat lunch?

B: On school days, I eat lunch at the school cafeteria.

A: What types of food do you usually have for lunch?

B: I usually have a sandwich, a slice of pizza, or some salad. I sometimes have a cookie after lunch.

ACTIONS

A: Do you like watching TV in the evening?

B: Yes, I enjoy watching TV in the evening after dinner.

A: What channels or programs do you watch?

B: I like to watch the Discovery Channel because it shows a lot of interesting programs about amazing things and places in the world.

A: Do you watch TV every day?

B: No, I usually watch TV only if I have finished all my homework. Sometimes, I only have time to watch TV during the weekends.

Now practice these dialogs with a classmate.

4 **Choose one of the questions below. Prepare your answer to this question by writing notes below. Use the questions from Part 3 to help with your notes.**

a. What time do you usually have breakfast? Who prepares it? What do you have for breakfast?

b. What time do you usually have lunch? What types of food do you usually have for lunch?

c. Do you like watching TV in the evening? What channels or programs do you watch?

Question: _____

My Notes

_____

_____

_____

Now interview two classmates. They will interview you as well. First, ask which question they chose. Then make notes of each answer.

My Classmates

Name: _____

Question: _____

_____

_____

Name: _____

Question: _____

_____

_____

5 **Tell your class about one of the classmates you interviewed.**

Example:

I talked to Ivan. He told me what he usually watches on TV in the evening. He said he has to do a lot of homework in the evening, so he only has time to watch one or two shows at night. One show he likes is a comedy about a crazy family. Another show he likes is about detectives solving crimes.

✔ **Rate your own speaking**

Information:	OK	Good	Excellent
Fluency:	OK	Good	Excellent
Pronunciation:	OK	Good	Excellent

6 Listen to each response and match it to the question it answers. 🔊 Track 27

a. What time do you usually go home after school?
What do you usually do when you get home?

b. Do you read newspapers, magazines, or books?
What do you usually read about?

c. What do you usually talk about with your family when you eat?

●   ● Response #1

●   ● Response #2

●   ● Response #3

For more practice, look at the transcripts on page 5 and practice these responses with a classmate.

7 Choose one of the questions below. Prepare your own response to this question by writing notes in the provided space. Be sure to explain your answer.

Question: _____

My Notes

_____

_____

_____

_____

_____

a. What time do you usually go home after school?
What do you usually do when you get home?

b. Do you read newspapers, magazines, or books?
What do you usually read about?

c. What do you usually talk about with your family when you eat?

Now share your response with a classmate.

 ✓ Rate your classmate's response:

	OK	Good	Excellent
Information:	OK	Good	Excellent
Fluency:	OK	Good	Excellent
Pronunciation:	OK	Good	Excellent

EXTRA PRACTICE

Try answering one or more of these questions for extra practice. Use at least three sentences in your response to each question.

1. How do you decide what to wear every day?
2. What is your day like after lunch?
3. Do you sometimes play games with your siblings or friends? What games do you play?
4. If you had more time, what would you really like to do?

Experiences

1 **Listen to the speakers. Write the questions that they answer.**  Track 28

a. **Speaker #1:** When was a time you _____ _____ _____?

b. **Speaker #2:** What is the best place _____ _____ _____?

c. **Speaker #3:** When do people _____ _____ _____?

2 **Sort the words by writing them in the correct categories.**

hard	letter	feel	country	sad
visit	remember	airport	exotic	high
university	study	happy	repeat	culture
proud	vacation	come		

DESCRIPTIONS

_____ _____ _____

_____ _____ _____

ACTIONS

_____ _____ _____

_____ _____ _____

THINGS

_____ _____ _____

_____ _____ _____

③ Listen to each dialog and read along. Track 29

 DESCRIPTIONS

A: Describe a time when you felt really proud of yourself.

B: I felt really proud of myself when I got the letter with my TOEFL iBT score because it was a good score.

A: Why were you so proud of this achievement?

B: Well, I studied really hard for the test, and I didn't want to have to repeat it because it is a difficult test.

A: What do you remember feeling when you got the letter?

B: I remember feeling both relieved and happy.

ACTIONS

A: What day of your life do you think you will remember forever?

B: I will always remember the day when I left my country to study abroad.

A: Describe the experience.

B: That day, my whole family and all my friends came to the airport to say goodbye to me and wish me luck.

A: Was it a happy day for you?

B: I was happy that I had the opportunity to study abroad, but I was also sad to leave my family and friends.

PLACES

A: Describe an experience you have had traveling to an exotic place.

B: When I was 14 years old, my family took me to Honolulu, Hawaii because we wanted to visit this exotic place and to have our vacation there.

A: What did you find interesting about Hawaii?

B: The colors all around us looked so different, and the culture was very different from my own.

A: What were the people like?

B: The people were very warm and friendly.

Now practice these dialogs with a classmate.

4 **Choose one of the questions below. Prepare your answer to this question by writing notes below. Use the questions from Part 3 to help with your notes.**

> a. Describe a time when you felt really proud of yourself.

> b. What day of your life do you think you will remember forever? Describe the experience.

> c. Describe an experience you have had traveling to an exotic place.

> Question: _____
>
> My Notes
>
> _____
>
> _____
>
> _____

Now interview two classmates. They will interview you as well. First, ask which question they chose. Then make notes of each answer.

My Classmates

> Name: _____
>
> Question: _____
>
> _____
>
> _____
>
> _____

> Name: _____
>
> Question: _____
>
> _____
>
> _____

5 **Tell your class about one of the classmates you interviewed.**

Example:

I talked to Jessica. She told me about a time when she felt proud of herself. That time was when she won an award in a contest. It was an English contest! She said that for that contest, she had to write a speech in English and give it in front of her classmates. She won first prize at her school.

✔ **Rate your own speaking**

Information:	OK	Good	Excellent
Fluency:	OK	Good	Excellent
Pronunciation:	OK	Good	Excellent

6 **Listen to each response and match it to the question it answers.** 🔊 Track 30

   a. Describe a situation when you felt really happy.   •   •   Response #1

   b. Describe an experience you had when you failed a test.   •   •   Response #2

   c. Describe an experience when you got something you really wanted.   •   •   Response #3

For more practice, look at the transcripts on page 5 and practice these responses with a classmate.

7 **Choose one of the questions below. Prepare your own response to this question by writing notes in the provided space. Be sure to explain your answer.**

   a. Describe a situation when you felt really happy.

   b. Describe an experience you had when you failed a test.

   c. Describe an experience when you got something you really wanted.

Now share your response with a classmate.

Question: _____

My Notes

_____

_____

_____

_____

_____

✔ **Rate your classmate's response:**

	OK	Good	Excellent
Information:	OK	Good	Excellent
Fluency:	OK	Good	Excellent
Pronunciation:	OK	Good	Excellent

EXTRA PRACTICE

Try answering one or more of these questions for extra practice. Use at least three sentences in your response to each question.

1. Describe an experience when you lied to somebody you love.
2. Describe a time when you saw a sunrise or a sunset.
3. Describe a close relationship you have with someone. Why are you so close to this person?
4. Describe a time when you were very nervous.

Family

1 **Listen to the speakers. Write the questions that they answer.** 🔊 Track 31

a. Speaker #1: Where do _____ _____ _____?

b. Speaker #2: What are your _____ _____?

c. Speaker #3: _____ _____ _____ does a typical family in your country have?

2 **Sort the words by writing them in the correct categories.**

perfect	annoy	celebrate	uncles	handsome
smart	husband	strong	grandparents	teach
get along	aunts	wife	live	tall
siblings	look up to	responsible		

DESCRIPTIONS

_____ _____ _____

_____ _____ _____

FAMILY MEMBERS

_____ _____ _____

_____ _____ _____

ACTIONS

_____ _____ _____

_____ _____ _____

3 **Listen to each dialog and read along.** 🔊 Track 32

💡 DESCRIPTIONS

A: **Who is your favorite sister, brother, or cousin?**

B: My favorite brother's name is Ali. He is my older brother. He is twenty years old.

A: **Why is he your favorite?**

B: I like him because he helps me and teaches me a lot of useful things.

A: **Describe him.**

B: Ali is very tall and strong. Everyone thinks he is handsome. He is also smart and responsible, so I really look up to him.

DESCRIPTIONS

A: **What is your idea of a perfect family?**

B: My idea of a perfect family is when parents, children, grandparents, uncles, aunts, and cousins all live close by so that they can help each other, spend time together, and celebrate together.

A: **Do your family members live near each other?**

B: Most of us live in the same city or close by. Some of my relatives live about an hour's drive away.

A: **Is there any family member who lives far away from the rest?**

B: Yes, my uncle and his wife live in Italy. We don't see them much.

🏊 ACTIONS

A: **Do you have any siblings or cousins?**

B: Yes, I have two siblings and three cousins.

A: **How old are they?**

B: My two older brothers are 15 and 17 years old, and my cousins are 7, 9, and 13.

A: **Do you get along well with your siblings?**

B: We all get along very well, though sometimes we get annoyed at my youngest cousin because he can get into things that he is not supposed to get into.

Now practice these dialogs with a classmate.

4 **Choose one of the questions below. Prepare your answer to this question by writing notes below. Use the questions from Part 3 to help with your notes.**

a. Tell me about your favorite sister, brother, or cousin.

b. What is your idea of a perfect family?

c. Do you have any siblings or cousins? If so, how old are they? Do you get along well with them?

Question: _____

My Notes

_____

_____

_____

Now interview two classmates. They will interview you as well. First, ask which question they chose. Then make notes of each answer.

My Classmates

Name: _____

Question: _____

_____

_____

Name: _____

Question: _____

_____

_____

5 **Tell your class about one of the classmates you interviewed.**

Example:

I talked to Larry. He explained his idea of a perfect family. He thinks that a perfect family should have two parents and two children. One child should be a boy and one child should be a girl. He told me that he doesn't have a perfect family. He has three brothers!

✔ Rate your own speaking

Information:	OK	Good	Excellent
Fluency:	OK	Good	Excellent
Pronunciation:	OK	Good	Excellent

6 **Listen to each response and match it to the question it answers.** 🔊 Track 33

a. What is the most important thing that your parents have taught you? •

b. What do you know about your great-grandparents? •

c. What holidays do you celebrate only with your family? Describe one. •

• Response #1

• Response #2

• Response #3

For more practice, look at the transcripts on page 6 and practice these responses with a classmate.

7 **Choose one of the questions below. Prepare your own response to this question by writing notes in the provided space. Be sure to explain your answer.**

a. What is the most important thing that your parents have taught you?

b. What do you know about your great-grandparents?

c. What holidays do you celebrate only with your family? Describe one.

Now share your response with a classmate.

Question: _____

My Notes

_____
_____
_____
_____
_____

Rate your classmate's response:

Information:	OK	Good	Excellent
Fluency:	OK	Good	Excellent
Pronunciation:	OK	Good	Excellent

EXTRA PRACTICE

Try answering one or more of these questions for extra practice. Use at least three sentences in your response to each question.

1. Talk about your parents. What is the best thing about your mother or father?
2. Who does the chores in your family? Who cleans, cooks, and does the laundry?
3. Should parents give their children an allowance? How much should it be?
4. Talk about one of your family traditions.

Feelings

① **Listen to the speakers. Write the questions that they answer.**  Track 34

a. **Speaker #1:** When do you _____ _____ ?

b. **Speaker #2:** When do you _____ _____ ?

c. **Speaker #3:** When do you _____ _____ _____ ?

② **Sort the words by writing them in the correct categories.**

angry	participate	notebook	receive	ashamed
change	impatient	quiz	present	grade
catch	birdhouse	embarrassed	situation	unfair
project	frustrated	build		

THINGS

_____ _____ _____

_____ _____ _____

ACTIONS

_____ _____ _____

_____ _____ _____

DESCRIPTIONS

_____ _____

_____ _____

FINAL EXAMINATION A+

Jonathon Doe, III
Spring Semester
Anytown High School

③ Listen to each dialog and read along. 🔊 Track 35

 THINGS

A: What things make you feel frustrated?

B: I get really frustrated when I try hard to accomplish something, and it does not come out the way I want it.

A: Why do you feel that way?

B: I feel like that because I am impatient.

A: Describe a situation when you felt like that.

B: Once I tried to build a birdhouse, but I couldn't get it right, so I got very frustrated and gave up. I ended up playing baseball instead. I was so frustrated that it felt good to hit the ball with my bat!

 ACTIONS

A: What things make you feel angry?

B: I feel angry when something unfair happens, and I can't change it.

A: Why do you feel that way?

B: I hate it when people are unfair to each other.

A: Describe a situation when you felt like that.

B: We were doing a group project at school, and one of the students was not participating enough. But after we presented the project well, we all received a good grade, including the student who didn't do much work.

 DESCRIPTIONS

A: What things make you feel embarrassed?

B: I feel really embarrassed when I do something wrong and someone sees me do it.

A: Why do you feel that way?

B: I feel like that because I know that what I am doing is wrong, and I feel ashamed when I am caught.

A: Describe a situation when you felt like that.

B: Well, for example, one day I was unprepared for a class quiz, so I decided to look in my notebook during the quiz. My teacher caught me doing it!

Now practice these dialogs with a classmate.

4 **Choose one of the questions below. Prepare your answer to this question by writing notes below. Use the questions from Part 3 to help with your notes.**

a. What things make you feel frustrated and why? Describe a situation when you felt like that.

b. What things make you feel angry and why? Describe a situation when you felt like that.

c. What things make you feel embarrassed and why? Describe a situation when you felt like that.

Question: _____

My Notes

_____

_____

_____

Now interview two classmates. They will interview you as well. First, ask which question they chose. Then make notes of each answer.

My Classmates

Name: _____

Question: _____

_____

_____

Name: _____

Question: _____

_____

_____

5 **Tell your class about one of the classmates you interviewed.**

Example:

I talked to Mary. She told me about a situation when she felt embarrassed. She said that once she wore her shirt inside out. Nobody told her about it all day! Finally, after she got home from school, her mother told her that her shirt was inside out. She was so embarrassed.

✔️ **Rate your own speaking**

Information:	OK	Good	Excellent
Fluency:	OK	Good	Excellent
Pronunciation:	OK	Good	Excellent

6 **Listen to each response and match it to the question it answers.** 🔊 Track 36

a. What things make you feel sad and why? Describe a situation when you felt like that.

•   •   Response #1

b. What things make you feel bored and why? Describe a situation when you felt like that.

•   •   Response #2

c. What things make you think a lot and why? Explain a situation like that.

•   •   Response #3

For more practice, look at the transcripts on page 6 and practice these responses with a classmate.

7 **Choose one of the questions below. Prepare your own response to this question by writing notes in the provided space. Be sure to explain your answer.**

a. What things make you feel sad and why?
Describe a situation when you felt like that.

b. What things make you feel bored and why?
Describe a situation when you felt like that.

c. What things make you think a lot and why?
Explain a situation like that.

Now share your response with a classmate.

Question: _____

My Notes

_____
_____
_____
_____
_____

✔ **Rate your classmate's response:**

	OK	Good	Excellent
Information:	OK	Good	Excellent
Fluency:	OK	Good	Excellent
Pronunciation:	OK	Good	Excellent

EXTRA PRACTICE

Try answering one or more of these questions for extra practice. Use at least three sentences in your response to each question.

1. What things make you feel tired and why? Describe a situation like that.
2. What things make you laugh and why? Describe a situation like that.
3. What things make you cover your eyes and why? Describe a situation like that.
4. What things make you blush and why? Describe a situation like that.

Air Travel

1 **Listen to the speakers. Write the questions that they answer.** 🔊 Track 37

a. **Speaker #1:** Have you _____ _____ _____ _____?

b. **Speaker #2:** What is the best way to _____ _____ _____?

c. **Speaker #3:** What can people do _____ _____?

2 **Sort the words by writing them in the correct categories.**

luggage	make	large	fly	compartment
domestic	airplane	boarding pass	specify	convenient
magazine	provide	early	arrive	visit
major	international	passport		

💡 **DESCRIPTIONS**

_____ _____ _____

_____ _____ _____

🤿 **ACTIONS**

_____ _____ _____

_____ _____ _____

📦 **THINGS**

_____ _____ _____

_____ _____ _____

DESCRIPTIONS

A: **What airline companies are there in your country?**

B: There are three major airlines in my country. One of them makes domestic flights. The other two provide international flights.

A: **Where do people from your country go by plane?**

B: People from my country fly to many other countries. For example, some people visit European countries, like France and Germany.

A: **Do you like traveling by air?**

B: Yes, I love traveling by air. It's fast and convenient.

ACTIONS

A: **How early should you arrive at an airport before a flight?**

B: You should arrive at the airport at least two hours before a flight.

A: **Why is this important?**

B: This is important because you need to have enough time to get your luggage checked in and to go through immigration and security with your passport, boarding pass, and carry-on luggage.

A: **Can these procedures take a lot of time?**

B: Yes, getting through security and immigration can take up a lot of time, especially during peak travel seasons.

DESCRIPTIONS

A: **Is carry-on luggage allowed on planes in your country?**

B: Yes, carry-on luggage is allowed on airplanes in my country, but it can't be very large.

A: **Why can't carry-on luggage be large?**

B: Carry-on luggage can't be too large because it has to fit in the overhead compartment or under the seat in front of you. Most airlines specify how big carry-on luggage can be, and people should follow these rules.

A: **What items do you like to have with you on an airplane?**

B: I like to have my iPod, my laptop computer, and a book or a magazine to keep myself occupied on long flights.

Now practice these dialogs with a classmate.

4 Choose one of the questions below. Prepare your answer to this question by writing notes below. Use the questions from Part 3 to help with your notes.

a. What airline companies are there in your country? Can you name some places where many people from your country go by plane?

b. How many hours do you have to arrive at an airport before a flight? Explain.

c. Is carry-on luggage allowed on planes in your country? What items do you like to have with you on an airplane?

Question: _____

My Notes

_____

_____

_____

Now interview two classmates. They will interview you as well.
First, ask which question they chose. Then make notes of each answer.

My Classmates

Name: _____

Question: _____

_____

_____

_____

Name: _____

Question: _____

_____

_____

_____

5 Tell your class about one of the classmates you interviewed.

Example:

I talked to Nick. He explained about two major airlines in his country. One of these is more popular and more expensive, but he said they are both pretty good. He also said that most people fly between the big cities in his country.

✔ **Rate your own speaking**

Information:	OK	Good	Excellent
Fluency:	OK	Good	Excellent
Pronunciation:	OK	Good	Excellent

6 Listen to each response and match it to the question it answers.  Track 39

a. Describe each section or class on a plane. • • Response #1

b. What are some safety features on a plane? • • Response #2

c. What situations can make a flight annoying? • • Response #3

For more practice, look at the transcripts on page 7 and practice these responses with a classmate.

7 **Choose one of the questions below. Prepare your own response to this question by writing notes in the provided space. Be sure to explain your answer.**

a. Describe each section or class on a plane.

b. What are some safety features on a plane?

c. What situations can make a flight annoying?

Now share your response with a classmate.

Question: _____

My Notes

_____

_____

_____

_____

_____

Rate your classmate's response:

Information:	OK	Good	Excellent
Fluency:	OK	Good	Excellent
Pronunciation:	OK	Good	Excellent

EXTRA PRACTICE

Try answering one or more of these questions for extra practice. Use at least three sentences in your response to each question.

1. On an airplane, would you prefer to sit by the window or by the aisle? Explain.
2. Are you afraid of flying? Explain.
3. Describe the responsibilities of a flight attendant.
4. After a flight, what do people do when they have arrived at their destination?

Food

1 **Listen to the speakers. Write the questions that they answer.** 🔊 Track 40

a. Speaker #1: What is _____ _____ _____?

b. Speaker #2: What is _____ _____ _____ you have tried?

c. Speaker #3: What does _____ _____ _____ in your country include?

2 **Sort the words by writing them in the correct categories.**

fantastic	spices	instructions	television	spaghetti
rice	dish	better	wonderful	kitchen
recipes	awful	meatballs	tasty	waffles
lasagna	cookbooks	appetizing		

INGREDIENTS/FOOD

_____ _____ _____

_____ _____ _____

THINGS

_____ _____ _____

_____ _____ _____

DESCRIPTIONS

_____ _____ _____

_____ _____ _____

3 **Listen to each dialog and read along.** Track 41

 FOOD

A: **What type of food do you like to prepare?**

B: I like to prepare a traditional dish that we eat in my native country. It is called Kabsa.

A: **Describe this dish.**

B: kielbasa is rice cooked with spiced lamb or chicken.

A: **Why do you like this dish so much?**

B: Well, it's quite easy to prepare. It also tastes wonderful because of all the different spices used in it.

THINGS

A: **Do you like to use recipes from cookbooks when preparing food?**

B: No, I don't. I never use recipes from cookbooks.

A: **Why?**

B: I have tried to use recipes from cookbooks several times, but they just don't work for me, even though I use all the right ingredients and follow the instructions. Either the food doesn't taste good, or it doesn't look appetizing.

A: **Tell me about your positive and negative experiences with cooking.**

B: Once I tried to make lasagna, but it tasted awful. However, I can make very tasty spaghetti and meatballs!

 DESCRIPTIONS

A: **Which of your parents is the better cook?**

B: My mom is a better cook than my dad.

A: **What is your favorite food that she makes?**

B: She makes really delicious waffles for breakfast. They are fantastic!

A: **Does your father also cook?**

B: No, he doesn't. As a matter of fact, I have never seen my dad in the kitchen cooking anything at all. My mom, however, is always there.

Now practice these dialogs with a classmate.

4 **Choose one of the questions below. Prepare your answer to this question by writing notes below. Use the questions from Part 3 to help with your notes.**

   a. What type of food do you like to prepare? Why?

   b. Do you like to use recipes from cookbooks when preparing food? Explain.

   c. Which of your parents is the better cook? What is your favorite food that he or she makes?

Question: _____

My Notes

_____

_____

_____

Now interview two classmates. They will interview you as well. First, ask which question they chose. Then make notes of each answer.

My Classmates

Name: _____

   Question: _____

_____

     _____

     _____

Name: _____

   Question: _____

_____

_____

_____

5 **Tell your class about one of the classmates you interviewed.**

Example:

I talked to Olga. She explained why she likes to use recipes from cookbooks. She says it is fun to cook and eat new things. By doing that, she said she has made some really tasty things. She also said she has made some awful things that she'll never cook again.

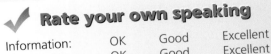

✔ **Rate your own speaking**

Information:	OK	Good	Excellent
Fluency:	OK	Good	Excellent
Pronunciation:	OK	Good	Excellent

6 **Listen to each response and match it to the question it answers.** 🔊 Track 42

   a. What food did you dislike as a child but have grown to like now?

     •   • Response #1

   b. What is your favorite dessert? Explain.

     •   • Response #2

   c. Do you think it is a good idea for parents to take their children to fast-food restaurants? Explain.

     •   • Response #3

For more practice, look at the transcripts on page 7 and practice these responses with a classmate.

7 **Choose one of the questions below. Prepare your own response to this question by writing notes in the provided space. Be sure to explain your answer.**

   a. What food did you dislike as a child but have grown to like now?

   b. What is your favorite dessert? Explain.

   c. Do you think it is a good idea for parents to take their children to fast-food restaurants? Explain.

Now share your response with a classmate.

Question: _____

My Notes

_____
_____
_____
_____
_____

Rate your classmate's response:

Information:	OK	Good	Excellent
Fluency:	OK	Good	Excellent
Pronunciation:	OK	Good	Excellent

EXTRA PRACTICE

Try answering one or more of these questions for extra practice. Use at least three sentences in your response to each question.

1. Who do you like to eat out with? Explain.
2. Do you think it is better to take friends to a restaurant or to a movie? Explain.
3. Is going on a diet good for a person's health? Explain.
4. What special foods do people prepare for celebrations and holidays in your country?

Fruits and Vegetables

1 **Listen to the speakers. Write the questions that they answer.**  Track 43

a. Speaker #1: What are _____ _____ _____ ?

b. Speaker #2: Have you ever _____ _____ _____ fruits or vegetables?

c. Speaker #3: What is _____ _____ _____ fruits and vegetables?

2 **Sort the words by writing them in the correct categories.**

favorite	onions	poisonous	limes	tangy
oranges	fresh	carrots	pineapples	beets
bananas	cabbage	sweet	lemons	broccoli
dangerous	apples	potatoes		

FRUITS

_____ _____ _____

_____ _____ _____

VEGETABLES

_____ _____ _____

_____ _____ _____

DESCRIPTIONS

_____ _____ _____

_____ _____ _____

3 **Listen to each dialog and read along.** Track 44

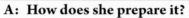

FRUITS

A: **What fruits do people grow in your country?**

B: Many farmers in my country grow fruits like bananas and pineapples. I guess citrus fruits are popular in my country. In some places in my country, you can see lots of orange, lemon, and lime trees.

A: **Name one of your favorite desserts made with fruit.**

B: My favorite dessert is orange ice cream.

A: **Describe this dessert.**

B: Well, it is usually made with fresh oranges, sugar, and milk. It is both sweet and tangy at the same time.

VEGETABLES

A: **What vegetables does your family usually put in soup?**

B: My grandma can make really delicious vegetable soup. She uses fresh cabbage, broccoli, onions, carrots, beets, potatoes, and spices.

A: **How does she prepare it?**

B: To prepare it, she puts all these ingredients in a pot and leaves it on the stove to cook overnight.

A: **What does it taste like?**

B: It's the most delicious vegetable soup in the world!

DESCRIPTIONS

A: **Do you think it makes a difference if fruits and vegetables are grown with chemical fertilizers and pesticides? Explain.**

B: Yes, it does make a difference because I think now we know a lot more about how chemicals can affect our health. There has been a lot of research in this area.

A: **How can chemicals and pesticides affect fruits and vegetables?**

B: Using pesticides keeps insects away from fruits and vegetables, but they can be dangerous to our health because pesticides are poisonous.

A: **Do you consider these things important when buying fruits and vegetables?**

B: Of course! When I buy fruits and vegetables, it is important for me to know where they came from and whether or not chemicals were used to grow them.

Now practice these dialogs with a classmate.

WARNING
PESTICIDE
APPLIED TO LAWN
HARMFUL TO PETS

4 **Choose one of the questions below. Prepare your answer to this question by writing notes below. Use the questions from Part 3 to help with your notes.**

a. What fruits do people grow in your native country? Name one of your favorite desserts made with fruit. Describe this dessert.

b. What vegetables does your mother or grandmother use to prepare soup? How does she prepare it?

c. Do you think it makes a difference if fruits and vegetables are grown with chemical fertilizers and pesticides? Explain.

Question: _____

My Notes

_____

_____

_____

Now interview two classmates. They will interview you as well. First, ask which question they chose. Then make notes of each answer.

My Classmates

Name: _____

Question: _____

_____

_____

_____

Name: _____

Question: _____

_____

_____

_____

5 **Tell your class about one of the classmates you interviewed.**

Example:

I talked to Paul. He explained why it is bad to grow fruits and vegetables using chemical fertilizers and pesticides. He said using those things can make people sick. Those chemicals and pesticides might not make people sick right away, but they may get sick when they get older.

✓ **Rate your own speaking**

Information:	OK	Good	Excellent
Fluency:	OK	Good	Excellent
Pronunciation:	OK	Good	Excellent

6 **Listen to each response and match it to the question it answers.** 🔊 Track 45

    a. Why do you think vegetarians choose not to eat meat? Would you consider being a vegetarian? Why?

    •   • Response #1

    b. What does this saying mean: An apple a day keeps the doctor away? Is it true?

    •   • Response #2

    c. If you were to create a new fruit or vegetable, what would it be? What would you name it?

    •   • Response #3

For more practice, look at the transcripts on page 8 and practice these responses with a classmate.

7 **Choose one of the questions below. Prepare your own response to this question by writing notes in the provided space. Be sure to explain your answer.**

    a. Why do you think vegetarians choose not to eat meat? Would you consider being a vegetarian? Why?

    b. What does this saying mean: An apple a day keeps the doctor away? Is it true?

    c. If you were to create a new fruit or vegetable, what would it be? What would you name it?

Now share your response with a classmate.

Question: _____

My Notes

_____

_____

_____

_____

_____

✔ **Rate your classmate's response:**

Information:	OK	Good	Excellent
Fluency:	OK	Good	Excellent
Pronunciation:	OK	Good	Excellent

EXTRA PRACTICE

Try answering one or more of these questions for extra practice. Use at least three sentences in your response to each question.

1. Why is it important to eat fruits and vegetables? How many should you eat each day?
2. What is your favorite fruit? Why? What dish can you prepare with your favorite fruit? How do you prepare it?
3. What does the saying "One rotten apple spoils the whole barrel" mean? Do you have a saying with a similar meaning in your culture?
4. What does it mean when someone is comparing apples to oranges? Explain. Do you have a similar saying in your culture?

Giving Directions

1 **Listen to the speakers. Write the questions that they answer.** 🔊 Track 46

a. Speaker #1: What is the easiest way to _____ _____ _____ _____ from school?

b. Speaker #2: Where is the _____ _____ _____ ?

c. Speaker #3: Where is a _____ _____ _____ ?

2 **Sort the words by writing them in the correct categories.**

grocery store	first	intersection	far	turn
left	give directions	bus stop	straight	walk
set up	traffic light	hospital	nearest	right
see	market	get off		

🏠 **PLACES/THINGS**

_____ _____ _____

_____ _____ _____

💡 **DESCRIPTIONS**

_____ _____ _____

_____ _____ _____

🏊 **ACTIONS**

_____ _____ _____

_____ _____ _____

🏠 PLACES/THINGS

A: You want your friend to visit one of your relatives with you. Give him directions from your home to your relative's home.

B: My Aunt Cecile's house is not far from my house, so you can walk there. First, go straight down Main Street.

A: What do I do next?

B: Then turn right onto Willow Drive. Walk two blocks until you get to the traffic light and turn left.

A: How will I know which house it is?

B: Aunt Cecile's house is number four. The front door is painted green.

💡 DESCRIPTIONS

A: You need some fruit and your friend offers to help you. Give him directions from your house to the nearest grocery store.

B: The nearest grocery store is quite far from here, so you will have to drive there. Go down Main Street and turn right onto Rosewood Road.

A: What do I do next?

B: Drive to the traffic lights at the intersection of Grant and Stone Street.

A: Is the grocery store on Stone Street?

B: Yes, turn left onto Stone Street, and you will see the grocery store.

🏊 ACTIONS

A: Your aunt is visiting from another city. You suggest she visit your local farmer's market on the weekend. Give her directions from your home to the market.

B: Our local farmers set up their market on Woodrow Street every weekend. To get there, you should take bus number two to Stanford Road.

A: Where do I get off on Stanford Road?

B: Get off at the first bus stop in front of the hospital, and walk two or three blocks along Stanford Road.

A: Where is the market?

B: You will see the market right next to the gas station on Stanford.

Now practice these dialogs with a classmate.

4 **Choose one of the questions below. Prepare your answer to this question by writing notes below. Use the questions from Part 3 to help with your notes.**

> a. You want your friend to visit one of your relatives with you. Give him directions from your home to your relative's home.
>
> b. You need some fruit and your friend offers to help you. Give him directions from your house to the nearest grocery store.
>
> c. Your aunt is visiting from another city. You suggest she visit your local farmer's market on the weekend. Give her directions from your home to the market.

Question: _____

My Notes

_____

_____

_____

Now interview two classmates. They will interview you as well. First, ask which question they chose. Then make notes of each answer.

My Classmates

Name: _____

Question: _____

_____

_____

_____

Name: _____

Question: _____

_____

_____

_____

5 **Tell your class about one of the classmates you interviewed.**

Example:

I talked to Rosa. She gave me directions from her house to her relative's house. First, you have to walk to a subway station. Then, you take the subway, but you have to transfer. When you get off the subway, you have to take a bus. It must be pretty far!

✔ **Rate your own speaking**

Information:	OK	Good	Excellent
Fluency:	OK	Good	Excellent
Pronunciation:	OK	Good	Excellent

6 Listen to each response and match it to the question it answers. 🔊 Track 48

    a. Describe how to get from your house to the nearest drugstore.   •   • Response #1

    b. Tell your friend where to find a dentist near his home.   •   • Response #2

    c. Describe how to go downtown by bus.   •   • Response #3

For more practice, look at the transcripts on page 8 and practice these responses with a classmate.

7 Choose one of the questions below. Prepare your own response to this question by writing notes in the provided space. Be sure to explain your answer.

    a. Describe how to get from your house to the nearest drugstore.

    b. Tell your friend where to find a dentist near his home.

    c. Describe how to go downtown by bus.

Now share your response with a classmate.

Question: _____

My Notes

_____

_____

_____

_____

_____

Rate your classmate's response:

Information:	OK	Good	Excellent
Fluency:	OK	Good	Excellent
Pronunciation:	OK	Good	Excellent

EXTRA PRACTICE

Try answering one or more of these questions for extra practice. Use at least three sentences in your response to each question.

1. Describe how to get from your house to school.
2. Give directions to the nearest supermarket from your house.
3. What is the fastest way to get downtown from your house?
4. Recommend a good place to get a haircut. Describe how to get there.

Health

1 **Listen to the speakers. Write the questions that they answer.** 🔊 Track 49

a. Speaker #1: What is one thing you learned _____ _____ _____ _____?

b. Speaker #2: What _____ - _____ - _____ _____ do you take?

c. Speaker #3: How often do you _____ _____ _____ _____?

2 **Sort the words by writing them in the correct categories.**

healthy	repair	restore	exhausted	bodies
allergy	help	important	vitamins	feel
injure	miserable	tasks	air	simple
tired	pollen	sneeze		

💡 **DESCRIPTIONS**

_____ _____ _____

_____ _____ _____

🤿 **ACTIONS**

_____ _____ _____

_____ _____ _____

📦 **THINGS**

_____ _____ _____

_____ _____ _____

3 **Listen to each dialog and read along.** 🔊 Track 50

 DESCRIPTIONS

A: **Why is it important to get enough sleep?**

B: Sleep is an important part of our lives because our bodies need sleep to restore ourselves after each day.

A: **What are some negative effects of not getting enough sleep?**

B: When we do not get enough sleep, we get exhausted easily and even simple tasks can seem difficult.

A: **How much sleep should you get each night?**

B: We should get at least eight hours of sleep each night.

 ACTIONS

A: **Why is it important to get enough vitamins?**

B: Getting enough vitamins is very important for our bodies because they need vitamins to be healthy.

A: **Why do our bodies need vitamins?**

B: Without vitamins, our bodies can't work normally.

A: **Describe one way in which vitamins help the body.**

B: Well, for example, vitamins can help the body repair itself when a part of it gets injured.

 THINGS

A: **Do you or any of your friends have allergies?**

B: Yes, I have a friend who is allergic to pollen.

A: **What is it like being allergic to pollen?**

B: In the spring, she sneezes a lot, and her eyes always water. Her nose gets very red, and she feels tired and miserable.

A: **Describe some other negative effects of having allergies.**

B: Because of my friend's allergy, she can't do activities outside when there is a lot of pollen in the air.

Now practice these dialogs with a classmate.

4 **Choose one of the questions below. Prepare your answer to this question by writing notes below. Use the questions from Part 3 to help with your notes.**

a. Why is it important to get enough sleep? What are some negative effects of not getting enough sleep? How much sleep should you get each night?

b. Why is it important to get enough vitamins? Explain.

c. Do you or any of your friends have allergies? Describe some negative effects of having allergies.

Question: _____

My Notes

_____

_____

_____

Now interview two classmates. They will interview you as well.
First, ask which question they chose. Then make notes of each answer.

My Classmates

Name: _____

Question: _____

_____

_____

_____

Name: _____

Question: _____

_____

_____

5 **Tell your class about one of the classmates you interviewed.**

Example:

I talked to Sam. He explained why it is important to get enough vitamins. He said that the body needs vitamins to work right and to stay healthy. He told me that one way to get enough vitamins is to take pills, but he doesn't do that. He said he just tries to eat lots of fruits and vegetables.

✔ **Rate your own speaking**

Information:	OK	Good	Excellent
Fluency:	OK	Good	Excellent
Pronunciation:	OK	Good	Excellent

6 Listen to each response and match it to the question it answers. 🔊 **Track 51**

a. What is your definition of "being healthy?" Explain.

•

•   Response #1

b. Do you think it is important to have health education classes in schools? Explain.

•

•   Response #2

c. Give examples of healthy eating habits. Do you think your eating habits are healthy? Explain.

•

•   Response #3

For more practice, look at the transcripts on page 9 and practice these responses with a classmate.

7 **Choose one of the questions below. Prepare your own response to this question by writing notes in the provided space. Be sure to explain your answer.**

a. What is your definition of "being healthy?" Explain.

b. Do you think it is important to have health education classes in schools? Explain.

c. Give examples of healthy eating habits. Do you think your eating habits are healthy? Explain.

Now share your response with a classmate.

Question: _____

My Notes

_____

_____

_____

_____

_____

✓ **Rate your classmate's response:**

	OK	Good	Excellent
Information:	OK	Good	Excellent
Fluency:	OK	Good	Excellent
Pronunciation:	OK	Good	Excellent

EXTRA PRACTICE

Try answering one or more of these questions for extra practice. Use at least three sentences in your response to each question.

1. Have you ever had a massage? Would you like to have one/another one? Why?
2. Give reasons why physical education (PE) classes are important.
3. Why is it important to take care of your teeth?
4. Give examples of bad habits that negatively influence people's health. Explain.

The Internet

---

1 **Listen to the speakers. Write the questions that they answer.** 🔊 Track 52

a. Speaker #1: Why do people like to _____ _____ _____?

b. Speaker #2: What can happen if you _____ _____ _____ _____ online?

c. Speaker #3: Should _____ _____ _____ to use the Internet?

---

2 **Sort the words by writing them in the correct categories.**

file	send pictures	at school	at home	download
in a library	buy things	research	website	coffee shops
program	access	post	Internet café	meet people
at work	send email	sell things		

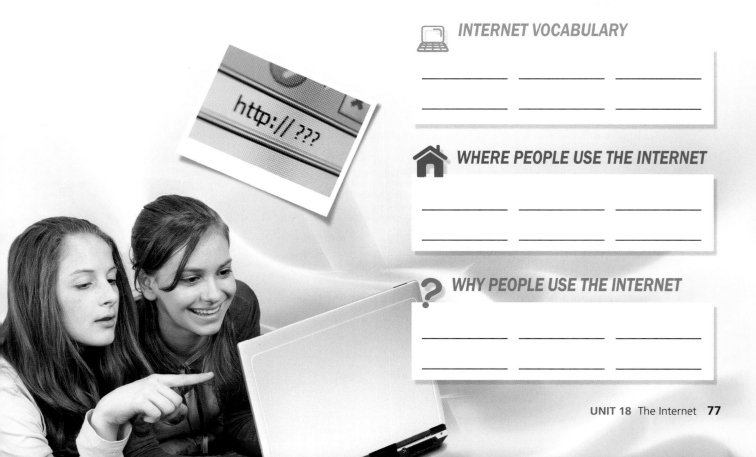

💻 **INTERNET VOCABULARY**

_____ _____ _____

_____ _____ _____

🏠 **WHERE PEOPLE USE THE INTERNET**

_____ _____ _____

_____ _____ _____

❓ WHY PEOPLE USE THE INTERNET

_____ _____ _____

_____ _____ _____

③ Listen to each dialog and read along. Track 53

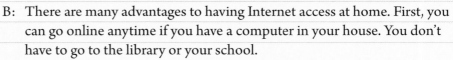

💻 INTERNET VOCABULARY

A: Why is it convenient to have and use email?

B: It is very convenient to have and use email because it is another fast and easy way to contact somebody besides using a telephone. All you need is an email program on your computer. Secondly, email is free, so you don't need to pay anything.

A: What are some of your favorite kinds of websites?

B: I really enjoy websites where I can talk to people from around the world. I like to leave posts to my friends on one website. It's really fun.

🏠 WHERE PEOPLE USE THE INTERNET

A: What are the advantages of having Internet access at home?

B: There are many advantages to having Internet access at home. First, you can go online anytime if you have a computer in your house. You don't have to go to the library or your school.

A: Have you ever used the Internet at the library or school?

B: Yes, I like to go on the Internet and check my email.

A: Where else have you seen people using the Internet?

B: I was in a coffee shop recently, and I saw several people using their laptop computers to access the Internet.

❓ WHY PEOPLE USE THE INTERNET

A: Describe how people use the Internet.

B: People use the Internet for various reasons. Some of them use it for business to communicate with their business partners in other countries, to send emails, business letters, and orders. Some people use it for personal reasons.

A: Have you ever bought anything online?

B: No, I have never bought anything online. My dad has bought many things online, and he has also sold lots of things for his home business.

A: Do you ever use the Internet for school?

B: If I have a research essay to write for school, the first place I go is the Internet. All I have to do is type my topic into a search engine, and I have all the information I need.

Now practice these dialogs with a classmate.

4 **Choose one of the questions below. Prepare your answer to this question by writing notes below. Use the questions from Part 3 to help with your notes.**

  a. Why is it convenient to have and use email?

  b. What are the advantages of having Internet access at home?

  c. Describe how people use the Internet.

Question: _____

My Notes

_____

_____

_____

Now interview two classmates. They will interview you as well. First, ask which question they chose. Then make notes of each answer.

My Classmates

Name: _____

Question: _____

_____

_____

_____

Name: _____

Question: _____

_____

_____

_____

5 **Tell your class about one of the classmates you interviewed.**

Example:

I talked to Theresa. She described how people use the Internet. She said most of her friends and family use the Internet for communication, like emailing or calling each other. Another way that she mentioned was using the Internet for research. She also talked about playing games online.

Rate your own speaking

Information:	OK	Good	Excellent
Fluency:	OK	Good	Excellent
Pronunciation:	OK	Good	Excellent

6 **Listen to each response and match it to the question it answers.** 🔊 Track 54

    a. What do you think of online classes or lectures?   ●   ●   Response #1

    b. What are the drawbacks of Internet use in education?   ●   ●   Response #2

    c. Do you think governments should control Internet access
       in their countries? Explain.   ●   ●   Response #3

For more practice, look at the transcripts on page 10 and practice these responses with a classmate.

7 **Choose one of the questions below. Prepare your own response to this question by writing notes in the provided space. Be sure to explain your answer.**

    a. What do you think of online classes or lectures?

    b. What are the drawbacks of Internet use in education?

    c. Do you think governments should control Internet access in their countries? Explain.

Question: _____

My Notes

_____

_____

_____

_____

_____

Now share your response with a classmate.

✔ **Rate your classmate's response:**

Information:	OK	Good	Excellent
Fluency:	OK	Good	Excellent
Pronunciation:	OK	Good	Excellent

EXTRA PRACTICE

Try answering one or more of these questions for extra practice. Use at least three sentences in your response to each question.

1. How can the Internet be improved? Provide specific examples.
2. How does the Internet help people do business all over the world?
3. Do you think the Internet can be addictive? Explain.
4. What information about yourself should you never provide online? Why?

Jobs and Occupations

1 **Listen to the speakers. Write the questions that they answer.** 🔊 Track 55

a. Speaker #1: What job would you _____ _____ _____ _____ ?

b. Speaker #2: What kind of jobs _____ _____ _____ ?

c. Speaker #3: What is _____ _____ _____ that one of your relatives has?

2 **Sort the words by writing them in the correct categories.**

accept	career	common	future	get a job
married	occupy	politician	position	president
require	responsibilities	satisfied	single	successful
take care of	traditional	travel		

PEOPLE/THINGS

_____ _____ _____

_____ _____ _____

ACTIONS

_____ _____ _____

_____ _____ _____

DESCRIPTIONS

_____ _____ _____

_____ _____ _____

③ Listen to each dialog and read along. Track 56

PEOPLE/THINGS

A: What are typical jobs for men in your country?

B: Men in my country occupy various positions. Common jobs for men are a police officer, businessman, doctor, firefighter, or politician.

A: Has there ever been a female president in your country?

B: No, in fact, no women have ever run for president in my country.

A: Do you think that a woman could be a good president?

B: I really believe that a woman could do a great job as my country's president.

ACTIONS

A: What is more important for women in your country: to have a career or to take care of their families?

B: Traditionally, it is more important for women in my country to take care of their families than to have a career.

A: Is that what your mother taught you?

B: My mother taught me that I could do whatever I wanted to do in my life.

A: Do you think that you will have a career or take care of a family?

B: Hopefully, I can have both a successful career and a successful family life, but it is hard to say what will happen in the future.

DESCRIPTIONS

A: Would you accept a job that required a lot of traveling? Explain.

B: Yes, I would accept a job that required a lot of traveling, as long as I was not married. After I got married, I would choose to spend more time with my wife and my children. As a single person, I would not have the responsibilities of supporting a family, so I could do more things that I wanted to.

A: Does your dad do a lot of traveling for his job?

B: No, he never has to travel for his job. He doesn't really like his job.

A: Is your dad planning on getting a new job in the future?

B: He's been talking about getting a new job for a while, and I think that he would feel more satisfied if he did.

Now practice these dialogs with a classmate.

4 **Choose one of the questions below. Prepare your answer to this question by writing notes below. Use the questions from Part 3 to help with your notes.**

a. What are typical jobs for men in your country?

b. What is more important for women in your country: to have a career or to take care of their families?

c. Would you accept a job that required a lot of traveling? Explain.

Question: _____

My Notes

_____

_____

_____

Now interview two classmates. They will interview you as well. First, ask which question they chose. Then make notes of each answer.

My Classmates

Name: _____

Question: _____

_____

_____

_____

Name: _____

Question: _____

_____

_____

_____

5 **Tell your class about one of the classmates you interviewed.**

Example:

I talked to Victor. He told me about the typical jobs for men in his country. He thinks that typical jobs for men in his country are the same as typical jobs for men in other countries. Men work in labor jobs or office jobs. He doesn't know any men who stay home and care for kids.

✔ **Rate your own speaking**

Information:	OK	Good	Excellent
Fluency:	OK	Good	Excellent
Pronunciation:	OK	Good	Excellent

6 Listen to each response and match it to the question it answers. 🔊 Track 57

    a. What is more important in a job, a good salary or working with nice, helpful people?

                    •   • Response #1

    b. What are the strategies for a successful job interview? Explain. •   • Response #2

    c. What are the advantages of being self-employed? •   • Response #3

For more practice, look at the transcripts on page 10 and practice these responses with a classmate.

7 **Choose one of the questions below. Prepare your own response to this question by writing notes in the provided space. Be sure to explain your answer.**

    a. What is more important in a job, a good salary or working with nice, helpful people?

    b. What are the strategies for a successful job interview? Explain.

    c. What are the advantages of being self-employed?

Now share your response with a classmate.

Question: _____

My Notes

_____
_____
_____
_____
_____

Rate your classmate's response:

Information:	OK	Good	Excellent
Fluency:	OK	Good	Excellent
Pronunciation:	OK	Good	Excellent

EXTRA PRACTICE

Try answering one or more of these questions for extra practice. Use at least three sentences in your response to each question.

1. If you had a choice, what would you choose to become? Why?
2. How do companies in your country reward workers/employees?
3. Where and how do you find a good job?
4. What is a workaholic?

Literature and Books

1 **Listen to the speakers. Write the questions that they answer.** 🔊 Track 58

a. Speaker #1: How often do you _____ _____ _____?

b. Speaker #2: Have you read a book that is _____ _____ _____?

c. Speaker #3: Why is it important to _____ _____ _____?

2 **Sort the words by writing them in the correct categories.**

newspapers	library	characters	park	living room
plot	labels	posters	settings	illustrations
comic books	school	bedroom	pictures	computer room
street signs	events	bus schedules		

THINGS TO READ

_____ _____ _____

_____ _____ _____

IN A BOOK

_____ _____ _____

_____ _____ _____

PLACES TO STUDY

_____ _____ _____

_____ _____ _____

3 Listen to each dialog and read along. Track 59

 THINGS TO READ

A: **Give examples of everyday activities that require good reading skills.**

B: There are many activities in our everyday life that require good reading skills. For example, we read newspapers to learn the news. We read labels on boxes, cans, and jars to know what we are eating. We need to read street signs so we don't get lost.

A: **Why is reading important?**

B: Reading is important if we want to learn something new.

IN A BOOK

A: **Is it important to have pictures, maps, and illustrations in books?**

B: Yes, it is. Pictures, maps, and illustrations give us a visual image of the main characters, events, and settings of books.

A: **Can there ever be too many pictures in a book?**

B: Yes, sometimes there are too many pictures. I still think the best part of reading a book is imagining things in the story.

A: **Can you think of any books that have lots of pictures?**

B: A lot of my school books have pictures, but that's because we need pictures to help us learn more about science and other subjects.

PLACES TO STUDY

A: **Why do some people prefer to study in the library?**

B: Some people prefer to study in the library because they can do research, or they can find more books on the subject that they are studying. Also, the atmosphere in the library is good for helping you focus on what you're studying.

A: **Where do you usually study?**

B: I usually study in my room at home.

A: **Why don't you study in the library?**

B: The library is too quiet. If I study there, I usually fall asleep.

Now practice these dialogs with a classmate.

4 Choose one of the questions below. Prepare your answer to this question by writing notes below. Use the questions from Part 3 to help with your notes.

   a. Give examples of everyday activities that require good reading skills.

   b. Is it important to have pictures, maps, and illustrations in books? Why?

   c. Why do some people prefer to study in the library?

> Question: _____
>
> My Notes
>
> _____
>
> _____
>
> _____

Now interview two classmates. They will interview you as well. First, ask which question they chose. Then make notes of each answer.

My Classmates

Name: _____

> Question: _____
>
> _____
>
>   _____
>
>   _____

Name: _____

> Question: _____
>
> _____
>
> _____
>
> _____

5 Tell your class about one of the classmates you interviewed.

Example:

I talked to Wilma. She explained why she likes to see pictures and maps in books. She said those pictures and maps help her understand the information or the story better. She thinks that she is a visual learner, so she needs pictures and maps to learn better.

✔ **Rate your own speaking**

Information:	OK	Good	Excellent
Fluency:	OK	Good	Excellent
Pronunciation:	OK	Good	Excellent

6 **Listen to each response and match it to the question it answers.** Track 60

    a. What is your favorite book? • • Response #1

    b. Who is your favorite writer? • • Response #2

    c. Where is your favorite library? How often do you go there? • • Response #3

For more practice, look at the transcripts on page 11 and practice these responses with a classmate.

7 **Choose one of the questions below. Prepare your own response to this question by writing notes in the provided space. Be sure to explain your answer.**

    a. What is your favorite book?

    b. Who is your favorite writer?

    c. Where is your favorite library?
       How often do you go there?

Now share your response with a classmate.

Question: _____

My Notes

_____
_____
_____
_____
_____

✔ Rate your classmate's response:

Information:	OK	Good	Excellent
Fluency:	OK	Good	Excellent
Pronunciation:	OK	Good	Excellent

EXTRA PRACTICE

Try answering one or more of these questions for extra practice. Use at least three sentences in your response to each question.

1. What is the last book that you read? Describe the plot.
2. Do you like reading classical literature? Why or why not?
3. What is one of the most famous books in your country? What is it about?
4. Do you think books will be important in the future or will the Internet replace them? Explain.

Just Speak Up

Olga Geissler

Transcripts

Answer Key

1

Unit 01 My Favorite

Track 1

❶ **Listen to the speakers. Write the questions that they answer.**

a. Speaker #1: My favorite teacher is Mr. Leonard. He is my science teacher. I think he explains things well, and he makes every science lesson fun.

b. Speaker #2: My favorite video game is *Pirate Treasure*. It is a game that you play online. You get to make your character and go on adventures. It's a lot of fun.

c. Speaker #3: My favorite sport to play is tennis. Tennis is better than other sport because you can play it at any time of year. You also only need one other person to play this sport. It's easy to find a friend to play with.

Track 3

❻ **Listen to each response and match it to the question it answers.**

Response #1: My favorite TV show is the sitcom (situation comedy) *Townhouse* because it is very funny. I think the characters are very original, and the dialog is very creative. It always makes me laugh.

Response #2: My favorite hobby is collecting coins. I like to collect coins and bills from different countries around the world. I always feel good when I get a new type of currency from another country.

Response #3: My favorite pets are dogs because dogs are very faithful and protective of their owners. Dogs are affectionate, and they actually like getting their owner's attention. Other pets are not as much fun as dogs.

Unit 02 My Country

Track 4

❶ **Listen to the speakers. Write the questions that they answer.**

a. Speaker #1: A famous food from my country is the candy called Chewy Bears. You may have tasted this candy. They are small jelly bears that taste like fruit. Kids all around the world love them.

b. Speaker #2: A really big company in my country is Star Technology. That company makes all kinds of things, from cars to televisions. In fact, I saw some products from this company when I visited my uncle in Australia.

c. Speaker #3: In my country, there are no real traditional clothes for men and women. Women and men generally wear casual clothes such as pants and shirts. For work or more formal situations, women and men both wear suits.

Track 6

❻ **Listen to each response and match it to the question it answers.**

Response #1: The best and the most popular restaurants are those that serve our more traditional food types. Seafood is very popular, as are different types of curry dishes. There is a big restaurant chain called Sea Harvest, which is very popular in my country.

Response #2: The main universities in my country are Central University, National University, and City University. They are located in the capital city, quite close to the center of the city. Of the three universities, National University is the largest.

Response #3: Yes, there are theme parks in my country. The most popular is Disney World, similar to Disney World in the US. It is very popular in my country. Sea World is also very popular, especially during the summer.

Studying English

Movies

Track 7

❶ **Listen to the speakers. Write the questions that they answer.**

a. Speaker #1: A good thing to do in class is participate actively. If you do this, you will most likely learn more from the lesson. So even if you don't like some activity or you think an exercise is boring, you should still try your best.

b. Speaker #2: It is important to do your homework because it is additional practice and reinforcement of what you are studying in class. If you don't do your homework, then you are more likely to forget what you learned in class that day. Your homework can also help prepare you for the next lesson.

c. Speaker #3: I learned to read English by using a computer game when I was five years old. My parents bought a CD-ROM for me and showed me how to use it. It was difficult at first, but with practice, it got much easier.

Track 9

❻ **Listen to each response and match it to the question it answers.**

Response #1: There are a lot of ways you can learn to read at a fast pace. The one that I know is to read a lot. You should read every day, and as you read, pay attention to the details in the book.

Response #2: Watching TV and listening to songs in English can help me improve my comprehension skills and help me learn new vocabulary. For example, when I watch TV in English, I often hear interesting words that I don't learn in books, as well as common expressions.

Response #3: The best way to learn new vocabulary is to read a lot because as you read you can recognize the new vocabulary words and observe how they are used in context. Another good way is to learn five words every day and try to use them when you talk to people.

Track 10

❶ **Listen to the speakers. Write the questions that they answer.**

a. Speaker #1: My favorite actor is Dustin Hoffman. I like him because he is able to play many different types of people. A lot of famous actors are simply themselves in movies, but Dustin Hoffman can seem like a different person each time.

b. Speaker #2: No, I don't like watching horror movies. I usually have nightmares after I watch them. I think some people enjoy being scared because they get a thrill from the excitement, but not me.

c. Speaker #3: An action movie is usually a fast, exciting movie where lots of things are happening. Usually, there is a hero who fights bad people. Famous action movies from my country include *The Myth* and *Fearless*.

Track 12

❻ **Listen to each response and match it to the question it answers.**

Response #1: I don't usually pay attention to movie ratings when I am choosing a movie to watch. Sometimes, I ask my friends what they thought of a particular movie, but if I am curious about one, I will just watch it. I'm old enough to watch anything.

Response #2: In my country, our movie industry has not developed very much. We have some small studios located close to our capital city. Most of our movies are made with actors from our popular soaps.

Response #3: No, I don't think young children should be allowed to watch horror movies. They can be really scared after watching these movies, and some younger children might not understand that things in the movies are not real.

Unit 05 Restaurants

Track 13

❶ Listen to the speakers. Write the questions that they answer.

a. Speaker #1: The last restaurant I went to was Burger World. I went there for lunch with my friends. I like that restaurant because it is not expensive and the food is good.

b. Speaker #2: When I eat out, I usually order iced tea to drink. I don't like drinking colas. They are too sweet, and I don't like the bubbles. Also, I think iced tea is better with a meal than water.

c. Speaker #3: Seafood is good for your health because it has good oil in it. I think it also has fewer chemicals in it than chicken or beef. Those kinds of meats can have lots of unnatural things in them.

Track 15

❻ Listen to each response and match it to the question it answers.

Response #1: I like to order dessert. I really like chocolate and fruit. Depending on my mood and if I am still hungry or not, I sometimes order a piece of fruit torte with chocolate.

Response #2: My favorite restaurant is the Golden Dragon, which is located on the corner of Main and 5th street. It serves Chinese food that is out of this world. The food is also very cheap, so we can go there every two or three weeks.

Response #3: When I go out, I like to try different restaurants, especially when I travel abroad because it gives me a chance to sample foods from different countries. If I find a really special restaurant, I will go more than once, or take friends there.

Unit 06 Music

Track 16

❶ Listen to the speakers. Write the questions that they answer.

a. Speaker #1: My favorite radio station is a sports station, not a music station. Sometimes this station plays music when there is not a game on, but most of the time they are talking about sports or broadcasting a game. I guess I'm not a big music fan.

b. Speaker #2: Yes, I like to sing with friends. One of the ways that young people spend time in my country is to go out and sing together. We do that a lot more than going places to dance. Some of my friends sing and dance, but I just like singing.

c. Speaker #3: The last time I bought a CD was probably two years ago. I quit buying CDs, and now I usually just download songs that I like. I think it's better to just buy the songs you like instead of buying a whole CD that might have some songs you don't like.

Track 18

❻ Listen to each response and match it to the question it answers.

Response #1: I like to sing, but I am not sure if I am a good singer. I like to sing at home when I do something that does not require concentration, like doing the laundry or taking a shower. However, whenever I sing in front of family members, they tell me to be quiet.

Response #2: I went to a concert last month, and I saw my favorite singer, Shakira. She was on a tour around the major cities of my country, and she visited my city as well. She sings Latin pop music. I liked the concert a lot because we could listen and dance.

Response #3: Music can help us learn English because it's one way to practice listening. For example, you can listen to songs in English and try to write down the lyrics. Also, when something is musical, it is much easier to remember the words.

Music is a good way to memorize English words and phrases.

Unit 07   **Name Them**

Track 19

① **Listen to the speakers. Write the questions that they answer.**

a. Speaker #1: The most famous artists that I know are van Gogh, Picasso, and da Vinci. All three of those artists are from Europe. I think their works of art can be found in museums around the world.

b. Speaker #2: Some popular magazines around the world are *Time, National Geographic,* and *Newsweek.* I've read some articles from all of those magazines. In fact, several of my English teachers used those magazines in their classes.

c. Speaker #3: A couple of really famous mountains are Mount Everest, Kilimanjaro, and Mount Fuji. Mount Everest is the tallest of those three mountains. I like hiking in the mountains, but I've never visited any of those mountains.

Track 21

⑥ **Listen to each response and match it to the question it answers.**

Response #1: Angelina Jolie, Sandra Bullock, and Julia Roberts are three famous actresses. Angelina Jolie is very famous because she is in a relationship with Brad Pitt. She also adopted a child from Africa, which is another reason that she is famous now.

Response #2: "Dirty Old Town," "The Lonesome Boatman," and "A Song for Ireland" are all popular songs in my country. I really like the song "Dirty Old Town" because it tells the story of a town in my country, and it is sung in our traditional style. It is still very popular with a lot of people.

Response #3: John Grisham, J. K. Rowling, and Dan Brown are three famous writers. Dan Brown is famous for *The da Vinci Code.* Both the movie and book were very famous. Many people were annoyed

by what the writer said in the book, which was another reason that it was famous.

Unit 08   **The Environment**

Track 22

① **Listen to the speakers. Write the questions that they answer.**

a. Speaker #1: One way to produce electricity is with the wind. These days, some companies make big windmills. When the wind makes the windmills turn, it produces electricity. I've seen pictures of big fields with lots of these windmills in them.

b. Speaker #2: A really bad effect of water pollution is that it kills fish. Of course, we shouldn't kill animals. That's bad. But when lots of fish die, that means there is less food for other animals that eat the fish. So, water pollution that kills fish can be bad for other animals as well.

c. Speaker #3: Global warming is a process where the Earth becomes hotter over time. These days, lots of people say that carbon dioxide in the atmosphere is causing global warming. Scientists are studying this, while other scientists are searching for ways to cut the amount of carbon dioxide humans produce.

Track 24

⑥ **Listen to each response and match it to the question it answers.**

Response #1: Cutting down trees causes major changes in the amount of oxygen that people and animals have available to breathe. Because trees consume carbon dioxide and produce oxygen, if we keep cutting down trees, we will increase carbon dioxide levels but lower oxygen levels.

Response #2: There are a lot of things we can do at home to save water. First, we can turn the water off when we are not using it, like when we brush our teeth. Second, we can reduce the amount of time we spend in the shower or in the bath.

Response #3: Yes, there is a lot of traffic in my

city. Traffic is a huge problem because traffic jams sometimes block the streets for hours. Pollution is a major concern. I think people should use their cars less frequently. They could also carpool to reduce the number of cars on the roads.

Unit 09 Everyday Activities

Track 25

❶ **Listen to the speakers. Write the questions that they answer.**

a. Speaker #1: I usually get up around six o'clock. It takes me about 45 minutes to get ready for school, so that's why I get up so early. Most mornings, I don't have time to eat breakfast.

b. Speaker #2: After school, I usually play a few computer games at home before I start my homework. I have to think a lot at school, so I need some time to relax after I get home. My mom only lets me play for about 30 minutes. Then, she tells me to start my homework.

c. Speaker #3: My typical weekend is not very interesting. I sleep late on Saturday and Sunday because I have to get up early all week. If I don't go out and meet my friends, I like to stay home and watch TV or DVDs. My family rents DVDs just about every weekend.

Track 27

❻ **Listen to each response and match it to the question it answers.**

Response #1: I usually go home at about 4:00 p.m. because I have to wait for a school bus to take me home. Right after I get home, I have a snack because I am usually starving by then. Then, I take a shower. Later, I watch television and do my homework.

Response #2: We usually talk about all sorts of things. Usually we discuss the events of our day, what happened, whom we met, and so on. We also try to plan activities to do during the weekend.

Response #3: Yes, I read newspapers and magazines all the time. I like to stay informed about the latest events at home and abroad. Also, I am a bit of a bookworm. I like reading biographies. I like books about famous people and historical events.

Unit 10 Experiences

Track 28

❶ **Listen to the speakers. Write the questions that they answer.**

a. Speaker #1: A time I was really scared was when the electricty went out in my apartment building. At that time, I was in the elevator! I thought I would be stuck there for hours, so I got scared. Luckily, the power came back on after a few minutes.

b. Speaker #2: The best place I ever visited was Paris. I had seen pictures of Paris, and I read a lot about it. Then, I got to go there with my cousin. We had a great time! It was just like I imagined.

c. Speaker #3: People usually get nervous before they have to do something in front of a lot of people. For example, if a person has to sing or dance on stage in front of people, he or she will probably be nervous before that. Or if a person has to give a presentation in class, he or she will be nervous then, too.

Track 30

❻ **Listen to each response and match it to the question it answers.**

Response #1: I felt really happy during my middle school graduation because I got the highest score in my class. It happened in May of last year. After my exams were over, my parents took my sister and me out for a nice meal to celebrate. It felt great because the celebration was for me.

Response #2: I was really happy on my 11th birthday because one of my dreams came true. I had been asking my parents to get me a puppy for a long, long time, but they kept saying no because they didn't think I was responsible enough to take care of a pet. When I finally got a puppy for my birthday, I felt great because I knew my parents felt I was responsible enough to take care of it.

Response #3: When I was 13 years old and in middle school, I failed a test because I was at a party the night before instead of studying hard. Even while I was taking the test, I knew I would fail because I didn't know any of the answers!

Family

Track 31

❶ Listen to the speakers. Write the questions that they answer.

a. Speaker #1: My grandmother lives in the same city as my parents, but she has her own apartment. My grandfather died a long time ago. Sometimes my parents worry about my grandmother because she lives alone. But my grandmother likes having her own apartment.

b. Speaker #2: My father has a job, and my mother is a housewife. My father works in a company that makes parts for computers. He is a manager there. Even though my mother stays at home, I think she has a full-time job, too. She has to take care of the house and do lots of stuff that my father can't do because he is at his office all day.

c. Speaker #3: The typical family in my country has one or two children. Most families I know have just one child, but it is not unusual to see a family with two children. Very few people have three or more children.

Track 33

❻ Listen to each response and match it to the question it answers.

Response #1: I know some facts about my great-grandparents because I was raised by my grandmother, who liked to tell me stories of when she was young. I know that they had a large family and owned a Chinese restaurant in the center of Hong Kong.

Response #2: The most important thing that my parents have taught me is how to be responsible. For example, when I was little and my parents bought me a puppy, my father taught me how to take care of it. I think I learned a lot about responsibility then.

Response #3: We celebrate anniversaries with our family. For example, last month, my grandparents had their 50th wedding anniversary, and we prepared a huge celebration for them. We booked a function room in a good restaurant and had all of our family members come for a nice meal.

Feelings

Track 34

❶ Listen to the speakers. Write the questions that they answer.

a. Speaker #1: I feel happy when I spend time with my friends. We usually do fun things together, so that makes me happy. One of our favorite things to do is to go bowling. We laugh a lot and have fun when we go bowling.

b. Speaker #2: I get annoyed when people on the bus start talking really loudly on their cell phones. I don't want to hear their conversations but they don't care. I would really like to say something to those people, but I never do.

c. Speaker #3: I never bite my nails, but my sister does. She bites her nails when she is worried about something. She seems to worry about a lot of things. Whenever I see her doing that, I tell her to stop it.

Track 36

❻ Listen to each response and match it to the question it answers.

Response #1: There are many things that bore me because I am very impatient, and I can't sit still when I am bored. For example, I was once at a presentation on how to be successful, and the presenter was quite boring. I wanted to leave after about five minutes.

Response #2: When I have to make a difficult but important decision, I usually think carefully about it because I do not want to make a mistake and then regret it later. For example, after I graduate from high school, I need to decide what major to choose for college. This is something I will need to make a careful decision about.

Response #3: I feel sad when something unfortunate happens to my family or my friends because I love them so much. For example, I felt really sad when my brother failed his math exam. He studied really hard for the exam, but it was very difficult.

Unit 13 Air Travel

Track 37

❶ **Listen to the speakers. Write the questions that they answer.**

a. Speaker #1: I have never been on a plane before. Many of my friends have flown on planes, so I have heard about the experience. Maybe someday in the near future I will get to fly somewhere.

b. Speaker #2: I think the best way to buy plane tickets is online. There are some good websites that offer cheap tickets to people. These days most people have e-tickets, so you don't even need to get a real ticket at all.

c. Speaker #3: During a flight, people can read magazines or watch movies. They can also listen to music. Some planes have small screens on the back of every seat. On those flights, people can even play video games.

Track 39

❻ **Listen to each response and match it to the question it answers.**

Response #1: There are many features that are designed to keep passengers safe on a plane. Flight attendants usually explain to passengers all the safety information before a flight, such as the way to put on oxygen masks and life jackets.

Response #2: There are many situations that can make a flight potentially annoying. For example, if your neighbor falls asleep and starts snoring, it can be very annoying. Also, when there is a crying baby near you, it can be difficult to relax.

Response #3: There are three sections on each plane: first class, business class, and economy class. First class is the most expensive. Business class is nearly as good as first class, though it is a little cheaper. Economy class is usually cheapest, but the seats are rather uncomfortable.

Unit 14 Food

Track 40

❶ **Listen to the speakers. Write the questions that they answer.**

a. Speaker #1: My favorite food is chicken soup with rice. I know that sounds kind of plain, but I love it. I like to eat this kind of soup on cold days when it is raining or snowing. It warms me up inside.

b. Speaker #2: The strangest food that I have tried is raw beef. I ate this in a restaurant near my house. My father told me that it was a traditional food from some country, but I can't remember which one. I didn't really like it, so I haven't eaten it again since then.

c. Speaker #3: The typical diet in my country includes lots of meat and potatoes in it. A long time ago, people would eat meat and potatoes at almost every meal. These days, there is more variety. But my family still eats meat and potatoes a lot, just not every day.

Track 42

❻ **Listen to each response and match it to the question it answers.**

Response #1: My favorite dessert is fruit torte because I love fruit. A fruit torte is a very rich cake with various kinds of fruit on top. My mom used to bake it for me when I was younger because I really like it. Now I can make it myself.

Response #2: No, I do not think that it's a good idea for parents to take their children to fast-food restaurants because we know that fast food is not good for our health. Also, if parents take their children there as a treat, they will be encouraging them to eat this type of food.

Response #3: As a child, I hated to eat vegetables, especially broccoli. My parents would keep saying, "Eat your vegetables. They are good for you." But I just didn't understand how anyone could like vegetables. Now that I am older, I love eating vegetables.

Unit 15 Fruits and Vegetables

Track 43

❶ Listen to the speakers. Write the questions that they answer.

a. Speaker #1: My favorite vegetables are carrots. They are a little bit sweet. I don't like cooked carrots as much as raw carrots. I like to eat crunchy carrot sticks with sandwiches.

b. Speaker #2: Yes, I have tried to grow vegetables. I did that as part of a science project for school. The teacher gave all of the students dried beans. We took the beans home and planted them. Then we watched to see if they would grow. Mine grew well until I forgot to water them for a few days. Then they died.

c. Speaker #3: The difference between fruits and vegetables probably has something to do with the part of the plant that we eat. Fruits usually have some kind of seeds in them, so they're related to the way plants reproduce. Vegetables can be leaves or roots or other parts of the plants.

Track 45

❻ Listen to each response and match it to the question it answers.

Response #1: "An apple a day keeps the doctor away" means that if you eat at least an apple a day, you will never need a doctor because this type of food keeps you healthy. I agree with the saying that

eating fruit is good for your body and will improve your health.

Response #2: I would create a mix between a plum and a tomato because I like the taste of both, and if I put those two tastes together, I think that would create an amazing new fruit. I would name it the plumato!

Response #3: There are many reasons why vegetarians may choose not to eat meat. First, there are religious reasons. Second, some people choose not to eat meat because they think that it is wrong to eat living creatures. Also, some people may not be able to eat meat because of health reasons.

Unit 16 Giving Directions

Track 46

❶ Listen to the speakers. Write the questions that they answer.

a. Speaker #1: The easiest way to get to my house from school is to take bus number 7. You can catch the bus at the corner of 54th Street and Parker Road. Get off the bus at the Palm Drive stop. My house is on the corner of Palm Drive and Parker Road.

b. Speaker #2: The nearest post office is next to the supermarket on Main Street. Just walk down the street from here and turn right at the traffic light. After you pass the supermarket, you will see the post office. You can't miss it.

c. Speaker #3: There is a good book store downtown. It's really big. If you take the subway, you can get off at the City Hall station. Then take exit eight out of the subway station. The book store is down the street at the next traffic light after you come out of the subway.

Track 48

❻ Listen to each response and match it to the question it answers.

Response #1: The drugstore is not far from our house, so you can walk there. First, go up River Road

and turn left onto Windy Lane. Walk two blocks and turn left onto Hanover Drive. The drugstore will be right in front of you.

Response #2: To get downtown from my house, you have to take bus number seven. The bus stop is two blocks down Oak Street. You will have to change two times, though. First, you change to bus number ten by the city hospital. When you get to Hanover Street, stop at the post office. Bus number 15 will pick you up from that bus stop and take you downtown.

Response #3: You'll have to drive to find the nearest dentist. From your home, you should drive to the intersection of Grant and Speedway and make a left onto Speedway. Then, pass the city zoo and turn right onto Wild Eagle Drive. Once you are there, you can't miss the dentist's building.

Unit 17 Health

Track 49

❶ Listen to the speakers. Write the questions that they answer.

a. Speaker #1: One thing I learned in physical education class was how to play volleyball. I really like playing volleyball, so I'm glad I learned it. I think it's fun to play volleyball at the beach.

b. Speaker #2: The only over-the-counter medication that I use is aspirin. Sometimes I take that if I have a headache or sore muscles. I might also take aspirin if I have a fever.

c. Speaker #3: I never go to the gym. It's too expensive. If I want to exercise, I just play basketball with my friends. Sometimes I also go jogging around the park for exercise.

Track 51

❻ Listen to each response and match it to the question it answers.

Response #1: Healthy eating habits include eating lots of vegetables and fruit, drinking water, and eating frequently in small amounts. Eating vegetables and fruit is important because they help the body grow. I think my eating habits are not as good as I would like them to be. Sometimes I eat unhealthy microwave snacks because they are fast and easy.

Response #2: My definition of being healthy is being physically and mentally fit. To be physically fit means to be the correct weight, not too skinny or overweight. To be mentally healthy means to have a clear mind and to be happy.

Response #3: Yes, it is important to have health education classes in school because children get a chance to learn about the human body, its growth, and its functions. Sometimes, parents do not have time or do not know how to explain some things about health and the human body to their children. health education classes, however, can teach children these things in a safe environment.

Unit 18 The Internet

Track 52

❶ Listen to the speakers. Write the questions that they answer.

a. Speaker #1: People like to use the Internet because it helps them do things faster. For example, if you have to find some information, you can find it really fast online. You can also shop faster by comparing prices at different stores. Of course, you can also use email to send messages to people really fast.

b. Speaker #2: If you spend too much time online, you can hurt your body. Your fingers and wrists can start having problems due to too much typing. You can also have back problems. Most people sit in a bad position when they use a computer.

c. Speaker #3: Yes, I think schools should allow students to use the Internet. In modern times, it is important for kids to learn how to use the Internet. They need to know how to find websites and use email. Schools can also teach them how to use the Internet wisely.

Track 54

6 **Listen to each response and match it to the question it answers.**

Response #1: I don't think that online education is of equal quality to education received in a regular classroom. I consider online education impersonal and uninvolved. I think students get more chances to deepen what they learn through talking with peers when they are in a classroom. Classrooms also provide competition to encourage students to try harder.

Response #2: No, I don't think that the government should control the Internet. The Internet is merely the sharing of ideas. The government has no right to control which ideas we can share and which ideas we cannot. The government cannot limit what we say on the telephone, so it should not limit what we can type. We should be allowed to access whatever we want on the Internet.

Response #3: There are many drawbacks to Internet use in education. However, I think the main drawback is people's inability to distinguish reliable, trustworthy information. If teachers do not teach students about proper Internet use, students might read something that is untrue. In addition, the Internet provides all sorts of distractions that can make it difficult for students to focus on their studies.

Unit 19   Jobs and Occupations

Track 55

1 **Listen to the speakers. Write the questions that they answer.**

a. Speaker #1: I would never want to be a doctor. Doctors have to work with sick people, and they have to see blood and gross things. Maybe they make a lot of money, but I don't care. I would never want to have a job like that!

b. Speaker #2: I have not had a real job in a company or anything. I have done some tutoring. I guess that counts as a job. When I was in high school, I tutored some of my neighbors in math. I usually did that once or twice a week.

c. Speaker #3: One of my relatives works for an oil company. For his job, he has to take a boat out in the ocean and live at the place where they are drilling for oil. He has to stay there for weeks or months at a time! I don't think that would be an easy job, but it seems pretty interesting to me.

Track 57

6 **Listen to each response and match it to the question it answers.**

Response #1: I think satisfaction, friendly people, and promotion opportunities are important in a job. It also needs to give you some sort of mental challenge. If that is not there, you will quickly become bored with the job.

Response #2: There are some advantages to being self-employed. If you are self-employed, you are your own boss. You can decide when you are going to take a vacation. More importantly, all the money that the company makes goes into your pocket.

Response #3: There are various strategies you need to keep in mind if you want to be successful at a job interview. First, do your homework. Research as much as you can about the company and the position you are interviewing for. It is also important to wear presentable clothing that is appropriate for the position.

Unit 20   Literature and Books

Track 58

1 **Listen to the speakers. Write the questions that they answer.**

a. Speaker #1: I rarely read for fun. I don't have much free time to read for pleasure. I have too much reading to do for my classes. If I have free time, I'd rather watch TV or play video games. I don't want to read unless I have to.

b. Speaker #2: Yes, I have. One book that I read and that was also made into a movie is *Jaws*. The book came out first. Then, the story was made into a famous movie. I think the director did a good job when he changed that story into a movie.

c. Speaker #3: It is important to read classical literature because people expect you to know about those stories. If you are talking to someone and they find out you don't know some classical work, they might assume you didn't do well in school. Or they might think you didn't even finish school!

Track 60

⑥ **Listen to each response and match it to the question it answers.**

Response #1: My favorite library is my city's main library, which is located close to my house. I typically go there about once a month. I normally check out books, but I can also check out magazines and DVDs as well.

Response #2: My favorite book is the travel book series *Lonely Planet*. I love these books because they give me great information. They have beautiful pictures as well as really important tips about getting around. They also have really handy maps that help me to know where I am going.

Response #3: My favorite writer is Dan Brown. He wrote *The da Vinci Code* as well as other books. He is able to combine suspense and a great story with historical evidence. When I start reading one of Dan Brown's books, I cannot put it down until I have finished it. He's a great author.

Unit 01 My Favorite

❶ Listen to the speakers. Write the questions that they answer.

  a. **Speaker #1:** Who is your favorite <u>teacher</u>?

  b. **Speaker #2:** What is your favorite <u>video</u> game?

  c. **Speaker #3:** What is your favorite <u>sport</u> to <u>play</u>?

❷ Sort the words by writing them in the correct categories.

People/Things: band, singer, subject, teacher, sports car, voice

Descriptions: important, beautiful, interesting, cool, powerful, fastest

Actions: speak, know, understand, drive, study, sing

❹ Choose one of the questions below. Prepare your answers to this question by writing notes below. Use the questions from part 3 to help with your notes.

Answers will vary.

  a. **What is your favorite school subject?**

  My favorite subject at school is English because I like studying it, and I know that it is very important for my future career. I will need to speak and understand English well because I want to work in tourism.

  b. **What is your favorite kind of car?**

  My favorite car is a Bugatti. It looks cool and is one of the fastest sports cars in the world. I think I would get a lot of attention from people if I drove one.

  c. **Who is your favorite band or singer?**

  My favorite singer is Shania Twain. I like the way she sings, and she has a very powerful voice. A lot of singers these days are famous because of their appearance, but she is both beautiful and talented.

❻ Listen to each response and match it to the question it answers.

  a. 2

  b. 3

  c. 1

❖ Extra Practice

Try answering one or more of these questions for extra practice. Use at least three sentences in your response to each question.

Sample Responses

1. **Describe your favorite friend and explain why he or she is your favorite friend.**

  My favorite friend is my best friend, Michael, because he is always honest, nice, and supportive. He is also very funny and makes me laugh. I have known him almost my whole life.

2. **Describe your favorite video or computer game and explain why it is your favorite.**

  My favorite computer game is *Football Hero*. It not only requires a lot of thinking but also good reactions. The music in the game is really good, too, with some popular new songs.

3. **Describe your favorite sporting event and explain why it is your favorite.**

  My favorite sporting event is Formula 1 car racing because I love fast sports cars and racing. I think there is a lot of skill involved, too. Some of the drivers are very talented.

4. **Describe your favorite job and explain why it is your favorite.**

  My favorite job would be to be a lawyer. Lawyers are responsible for finding the truth and ensuring that people are brought to justice. They also protect people's rights.

Unit 02 My Country

❶ Listen to the speakers. Write the questions that they answer.

  a. **Speaker #1:** What is a <u>famous</u> <u>food</u> from your country?

b. **Speaker #2:** What is a <u>big company</u> in your country?

c. **Speaker #3:** What are <u>traditional clothes</u> in your country?

❷ **Sort the words by writing them in the correct categories.**

Actions: hold on to, speak, immigrate, grow, hear, live

Things/People: architecture, capital, territory, foreigner, population, size

Descriptions: native, official, large, the same as, less than, well known

❹ **Choose one of the questions below. Prepare your answers to this question by writing notes below. Use the questions from part 3 to help with your notes.**

Answers will vary.

a. **How big is your native country? How many people live there?**

The territory of my native country isn't very large. It is probably the same size as Germany. There are less than five million people in my country. I think a lot of foreigners have started immigrating to my country in recent years.

b. **What are the official languages of your native country?**

There are two official languages in my country. They are Irish and English. English is spoken throughout the country, but in some parts, people speak Irish. You might hear people speaking Polish and Chinese. There are lots of people from Poland and China in my country.

c. **What is the capital city of your country? Is this city known for anything?**

The capital city of my country is Rome. It is a very old but very beautiful city. It is located in the west of the country. Rome is well known for its architecture and the fact that it has held on to many old traditions.

❻ **Listen to each response and match it to the question it answers.**

a. 2

b. 1

c. 3

❖ **Extra Practice**

Try answering one or more of these questions for extra practice. Use at least three sentences in your response to each question.

Sample Responses

1. **Describe the culture and traditions in your native country.**

People of my native country are proud of their culture and traditions. We are famous for having fun and also doing a certain type of dance. We try to preserve the traditions of our country by sending children to summer camps where they learn the old language and traditions.

2. **What are the traditional clothes in your native country?**

The traditional clothes for women in my country look like long dresses that have pretty patterns on them. Usually women only wear these for special occasions like weddings. There used to be a traditional dress for men as well, but men these days don't wear it anymore.

3. **Where can people see performances or enjoy the circus in your native country?**

There are theaters, opera houses, and circus buildings in my country. Many of them are located in the center of the city. Some cheaper ones are located in areas where students stay.

4. **What are the most popular vacation destinations in your country?**

The most popular vacation destinations in my country are the big cities. There are two big cities, one in the north and one in the south, that most people visit. If people go to other places in my country, they'll probably only see small farming villages.

Unit 03　Studying English

❶ Listen to the speakers. Write the questions that they answer.

   a. Speaker #1: What is a good thing to <u>do in class</u>?

   b. Speaker #2: Why is it important to <u>do your homework</u>?

   c. Speaker #3: How did you learn to <u>read English</u>?

❷ Sort the words by writing them in the correct categories.

   Actions: master, pronounce, focus on, watch, improve, practice

   People: students, native speakers, teachers, friends, others, parents

   Things: definition, sentences, songs, tenses, grammar, straight As

❹ Choose one of the questions below. Prepare your answers to this question by writing notes below. Use the questions from part 3 to help with your notes.

   Answers will vary.

   a. Do you think it is important to study English grammar?

   Yes, studying English grammar is very important for mastering English. You should especially focus on studying tenses. This way you can learn to form more sentences in different tenses.

   b. What do you think the best ways to practice speaking English are?

   There are a lot of ways to practice speaking English. First, you should find every chance to speak English. You can practice speaking with your friends, teachers, or native speakers. You should also watch English TV and listen to English songs. That can help you learn how to pronounce words correctly.

   c. What is your definition of a "good student?"

   My definition of a good student is a student who

tries hard. In my opinion, a good student is not necessarily a straight A student. As long as others, like parents and teachers, can see that the student is trying hard to improve, then that student fits my definition of a "good student."

❻ Listen to each response and match it to the question it answers.

   a. 1

   b. 3

   c. 2

❖ Extra Practice

Try answering one or more of these questions for extra practice. Use at least three sentences in your response to each question.

Sample Responses

1. Why is it important to be on time for class?

   When students are on time for class, they get a chance to prepare for their classes calmly, to concentrate on their subjects, and to show respect for their teachers and classmates. When students are late, they aren't prepared and may have missed something important at the beginning of the class.

2. What should you do and not do in class?

   There are a lot of things you should do and a lot of things you should not do in class. First, you should come to class on time, come prepared, pay attention in class, and participate actively in activities and assignments. If you do all these things, you will most likely be successful in your studies. What you should not do is ignore this advice.

3. Why is it important to do your homework regularly?

   It is important to do your homework regularly because it is additional practice and reinforcement of what you are studying in class. If you don't do your homework, then you are more likely to forget what you learned in class that day.

4. How did you learn to read English? Do you think it was easy or difficult?

I learned to read English by using one of those phonics instructional workbook series when I was five years old. My parents bought this series for me and showed me how to use it. It was difficult at first, but with practice it got much easier.

Unit 04 Movies

❶ Listen to the speakers. Write the questions that they answer.

a. **Speaker #1:** Who is your <u>favorite</u> <u>actor</u>?

b. **Speaker #2:** Do you like <u>horror</u> <u>movies</u>?

c. **Speaker #3:** What is an <u>action</u> <u>movie</u>?

❷ Sort the words by writing them in the correct categories.

Things: membership card, price, tickets, drive-in, screen, sound system

Times: always, months before, usually, never, every weekend, often

Descriptions: cheaper, rainy, expensive, new, wide, fun

❹ Choose one of the questions below. Prepare your answers to this question by writing notes below. Use the questions from part 3 to help with your notes.

Answers will vary.

a. **Do you like going to the movies? Explain.**

Yes, I really enjoy going to see movies. I usually go with my friends every other weekend. We have membership cards, so we always get tickets for the movies at a cheaper price.

b. **What are the advantages and disadvantages of watching a movie in a movie theater?**

The advantages are the wide screen and the sound system that is used. Also, you usually see movies in a movie theater months before they come out on TV. One disadvantage is that it is expensive. Also, sometimes people make noise and ruin the movie.

c. **Are drive-in movie theaters popular in your country?**

No, I don't actually think there are any drive-in movie theaters in my country. This is probably because the weather is not very nice. It's rainy and cold outdoors quite often. No, I've never been to a drive-in movie theater. I don't think it would be fun to see a movie there, anyway.

❻ Listen to each response and match it to the question it answers.

a. 1

b. 3

c. 2

❖ **Extra Practice**

Try answering one or more of these questions for extra practice. Use at least three sentences in your response to each question.

Sample Responses

1. **Who is your favorite actor/actress? Why?**

My favorite actress is Meryl Streep. I like her because she is able to play many different types of people. A lot of famous actresses are simply themselves in movies, but Meryl Streep can seem like a different person each time.

2. **Why do some people like watching horror movies?**

I don't like watching horror movies. I usually have nightmares after I watch them. I think some people enjoy being scared because they get a thrill from the excitement.

3. **Do you think animated movies are only for children? Explain.**

No, I don't think animated movies are only for children. In Japan, many animated movies are produced for adults. These are often very scary and should only be watched by people over a certain age.

4. **What is an action movie? Give examples of famous action movies in your country.**

An action movie is usually a fast, exciting movie where lots of things are happening. Actions movies usually have lots of car chases or shooting scenes. A famous action movie from my country is *The Flying Dragon*.

Unit 05 Restaurants

❶ **Listen to the speakers. Write the questions that they answer.**

a. **Speaker #1:** What was the <u>last</u> <u>restaurant</u> you went to?

b. **Speaker #2:** What <u>drink</u> do you usually order when you eat out?

c. **Speaker #3:** Why is <u>seafood</u> good for your health?

❷ **Sort the words by writing them in the correct categories.**

Things: appetizer, main course, spring rolls, meal, noodle, opportunity

Actions: cook, prefer, prepare, travel, sample, order

Descriptions: particular, traditional, different, healthier, various, homemade

❹ **Choose one of the questions below. Prepare your answers to this question by writing notes below. Use the questions from part 3 to help with your notes.**

Answers will vary.

a. **Do you prefer to eat out or to eat at home? Explain.**

Maybe I am too traditional, but I prefer to eat at home. I enjoy the company of my family and the quality time we have together. I like it when we prepare our homemade food and eat it together. I'm sure the meals are healthier that way.

b. **When you eat out, do you like to order appetizers? If so, what?**

Yes, I like to order different kinds of appetizers when I eat out. I like to sample various things before I have my main course. It depends on the kind of a restaurant I go to, but I usually have spring rolls. A good restaurant for spring rolls is the Vietnamese noodle house near my apartment.

c. **Is it a good idea to eat out when you travel to other countries? Explain.**

Of course! I think people should use the opportunity to sample food from different countries when they travel abroad because it is one way to learn about various cultures in other countries. Another good reason for eating out when you travel is so that you don't have to cook. Who wants to cook when they're on vacation? Not me!

❻ **Listen to each response and match it to the question it answers.**

a. 2

b. 1

c. 3

❖ **Extra Practice**

Try answering one or more of these questions for extra practice. Use at least three sentences in your response to each question.

Sample Responses

1. **What is a traditional food in your culture? How is it prepared?**

Lamb stew is a traditional food in my culture. To prepare it, you need to put lamb, onions, carrots and leeks in a pot. Then you let it cook on a low heat for several hours. It is really delicious and very popular.

2. **When you go to your favorite restaurant, what do you usually order? Why?**

When I go to my favorite Italian restaurant, the Olive Garden, I usually order its house salad because it is so delicious and healthy. I also like to order their bolognaise, which is much more exciting than regular bolognaise.

3. Do you like to eat at fast-food restaurants? Why or why not?

No. I don't. When I was very young, I thought eating in a fast-food restaurant was a treat. Now I know that fast food is very unhealthy, so I never eat it.

4. Describe a bad experience that you had in a restaurant.

Once I was at a Mexican restaurant because I really wanted to try some Mexican food. I can't eat really spicy food, and the food that I ordered was very spicy, so it made me really sick. I didn't know that it would do that to me.

Unit 06 **Music**

❶ **Listen to the speakers. Write the questions that they answer.**

a. **Speaker #1:** What is your favorite <u>radio</u> <u>station</u>?

b. **Speaker #2:** Do you like to <u>sing</u> <u>with</u> <u>friends</u>?

c. **Speaker #3:** When was the last time you <u>bought</u> <u>a</u> <u>CD</u>?

❷ **Sort the words by writing them in the correct categories.**

Kinds of Music: classical music, heavy metal, rap music, jazz, dance music, Latin pop

Descriptions: annoying, energetic, wonderful, young, distracting, loud

Things: piano, situation, sound, club, saxophone, school

❹ **Choose one of the questions below. Prepare your answers to this question by writing notes below. Use the questions from part 3 to help with your notes.**

Answers will vary.

a. **What is your favorite kind of music? What do you like about it?**

My favorite kind of music is Latin pop because

it is the music that I grew up with. Latin pop is mostly used as dance music, so it is played in dance clubs. It is energetic, so it makes me want to dance. I really like dancing.

b. **Do you play any musical instruments? If so, how long have you been playing?**

Yes, I do. I play the piano. I like playing classical music on the piano. My parents took me to a music school when I was very young. I guess I was about seven when I started learning to play the piano. I would love to learn to play the saxophone because I think it has a wonderful sound.

c. **Describe a situation when music can be distracting.**

Music can be distracting when it is too loud. Loud rap music or heavy metal can be very annoying. Even when somebody is playing jazz, my favorite kind of music, if it is too loud, I still wouldn't enjoy it. It would bother me. Music can also be very distracting when you are doing homework.

❻ **Listen to each response and match it to the question it answers.**

a. 1

b. 3

c. 2

❖ **Extra Practice**

Try answering one or more of these questions for extra practice. Use at least three sentences in your response to each question.

Sample Responses

1. **Describe how music can influence your mood.**

Music can influence my mood a lot. For example, when I am sad or just tired, I play some disco music and start dancing. My mood changes very quickly, and I usually feel a lot better.

2. **How is your taste in music different from your parents'? Give examples.**

My taste in music is very different from

my parents' because I like rap and hip-hop, whereas they listen to classical music. The type of music I listen to is very energetic, while I think classical music is quite boring.

3. What is your favorite style of dancing? Are you good at it? Explain.

I like salsa a lot. It is a traditional Latin American style of dancing. It is very exciting. I am not good at it since I have never taken lessons, but I enjoy doing it anyway.

4. What is your favorite radio station? When do you listen to it?

My favorite radio station is Radio 7 because they broadcast music that is popular with young people now. They don't play any outdated or oldies songs. I usually listen to it when I am studying or jogging.

Unit 07 **Name Them**

❶ **Listen to the speakers. Write the questions that they answer.**

a. Speaker #1: Who are some <u>famous</u> <u>artists</u>?

b. Speaker #2: What are some <u>popular</u> <u>magazines</u>?

c. Speaker #3: What are some <u>famous</u> <u>mountains</u>?

❷ **Sort the words by writing them in the correct categories.**

Things: meter, sights, tower, ending, 100 meter sprint, record

Places: China, Paris, heaven, India, Los Angeles, Windsor Palace

Actions: visit, read, talk about, win, recommend, tell

❹ **Choose one of the questions below. Prepare your answers to this question by writing notes below. Use the questions from part 3 to help with your notes.**

Answers will vary.

a. What are the titles of some famous books? Have you read any of these books?

Some famous books that I know are *The Alchemist, The Five People You Meet in Heaven*, and *Life of Pi*. I read *Life of Pi*. It is a very interesting book about a boy from India and a tiger. It has a very good ending. I would highly recommend this book.

b. What are some famous cities in the world? Describe one of them.

The most famous cities in the world are Los Angeles, New York, London, Paris, and Tokyo. I visited London once. It is best known for sights like Big Ben, Windsor Palace, and the Tower of London. It is one of the largest cities in the world. Maybe about 14 million people live there.

c. Who are some famous athletes? Describe one of them.

Some famous athletes these days are Michael Phelps, Usain Bolt, and Kelly Holmes. Usain Bolt is famous because he won the Olympics in China. He set a new world record for the 100-meter sprint. He is kind of unusual because he is so tall and sprinters are not usually that tall.

❻ **Listen to each response and match it to the question it answers.**

a. 1

b. 2

c. 3

❖ **Extra Practice**

Try answering one or more of these questions for extra practice. Use at least three sentences in your response to each question.

Sample Responses

1. Give the names of three famous actors and talk about one of them.

Some of the most famous actors in the world are Brad Pitt, Johnny Depp, and George Clooney. Brad Pitt is well known for *Mr. and Mrs. Smith*, which is about two professional killers who are married.

The movie also starred Angelina Jolie. Brad Pitt is famous because he's very good looking, and he's a pretty good actor.

2. **Give the names of three famous singers and talk about one of them.**

Three famous singers are Michael Jackson, Elton John, and Celine Dion. Michael Jackson is best known for his album *Thriller,* which sold millions of copies in the early 1980s. Some other interesting things about him are that he owned a monkey, lived in an amusement park, and had some trouble with the law.

3. **Give the titles of three famous movies and talk about one of them.**

Lord of the Rings, Harry Potter, and *Jerry Maguire* are three famous movies. *Lord of the Rings* is one of my favorite movies because the special effects are amazing. I really like the book, so I was happy when the movie was just as good.

4. **Give the titles of three famous TV shows and talk about one of them.**

Lost, 24, and *Scrubs* are all good TV shows. I really like *Lost* because it is very interesting. It is about an airplane that crashed on an island and all the people realize that something strange is happening on the island. They see very strange things and meet other people on the island.

Unit 08 **The Environment**

❶ **Listen to the speakers. Write the questions that they answer.**

a. **Speaker #1:** What is one way to <u>produce</u> <u>electricity</u>?

b. **Speaker #2:** What is an effect of <u>water</u> <u>pollution</u>?

c. **Speaker #3:** What is <u>global</u> <u>warming</u>?

❷ **Sort the words by writing them in the correct categories.**

Nature: plants, land, streams, trees, rivers, animals

Actions: grow, drink, recycle, collect, produce, pollute

Materials: glass, paper, cloth, cardboard, plastic, metal

❹ **Choose one of the questions below. Prepare your answers to this question by writing notes below. Use the questions from part 3 to help with your notes.**

Answers will vary.

a. **Why is it dangerous for the environment when cities grow and take up more land?**

It is harmful for the environment because there is less land available for trees and other plants to grow, and for animals to live. Fewer plants mean less oxygen is produced. Since all living things need oxygen to survive, of course this is bad.

b. **What are the effects of polluting water? Explain.**

Our water comes from rivers and streams. The main danger of polluting this water is that people have to use or drink it. If there is too much pollution in streams, the amount of available fresh water will not be enough for everyone to drink.

c. **What household items can be recycled? What do you collect at home for recycling?**

We can recycle paper, cardboard, cloth, plastic, metal, and glass. For recycling, my family and I collect old newspapers, magazines, old clothes, milk cartons, plastic containers, and aluminum cans. Recycling is important because it means that we can reuse a lot of things. This conserves resources.

❻ **Listen to each response and match it to the question it answers.**

a. 3

b. 2

c. 1

❖ **Extra Practice**

Try answering one or more of these questions for extra practice. Use at least three sentences in your response to each question.

Sample Responses

1. Why is it important to use electricity wisely? Explain.

It is important to use electricity wisely because it is very expensive to produce, and lots of natural resources are being used to generate it. For example, to generate electricity, we need to burn coal or natural gas. So if we waste electricity, we need to burn more coal and gas which pollutes the environment.

2. What national parks and nature reserves do you have in your country?

We have a lot of national parks and nature reserves in our country. They are important for preserving nature in all its beauty. The biggest one is Yellowstone. In particular, it preserves many species of trees, bears, and big game.

3. Why is it important for people to clean up garbage in picnic areas before they leave?

It is very important to clean up the garbage in picnic areas because it pollutes nature and creates an unpleasant environment in those areas. Also, garbage can attract dangerous wild animals such as bears.

4. What can children do to help preserve the environment?

Children can do a lot of things to help preserve the environment. First, they need to learn not to litter, and if they see garbage in the street, they should learn to pick it up. Also, they can make sure that they recycle all the materials they use.

Unit 09 Everyday Activities

❶ Listen to the speakers. Write the questions that they answer.

a. Speaker #1: What time do you <u>get up</u>?

b. Speaker #2: What do you do <u>after school</u>?

c. Speaker #3: What do you do on <u>a typical weekend</u>?

❷ Sort the words by writing them in the correct categories.

Meals/Mealtimes: breakfast, evening, dinner, morning, noon, lunch

Food: cookie, pizza, oatmeal, bread, pancakes, salad

Actions: eat, relax, watch, leave, cook, show

❹ Choose one of the questions below. Prepare your answers to this question by writing notes below. Use the questions from part 3 to help with your notes.

Answers will vary.

a. What time do you usually have breakfast? Who prepares it? What do you have for breakfast?

I usually have my breakfast at around seven o'clock in the morning. My mom usually cooks it for me, but when she has to go to work early, I make breakfast myself. I usually have bread or oatmeal. On weekends, I have pancakes!

b. What time do you usually have lunch? What types of food do you usually have for lunch?

I usually have lunch at around noon. Because I have breakfast at seven, I am usually very hungry by then. On school days, I eat lunch at the school cafeteria. I usually have a sandwich, a slice of pizza, or some salad. I sometimes have a cookie after lunch.

c. Do you like watching TV in the evening? What channels or programs do you watch?

Yes, I enjoy watching TV in the evening after dinner. I like to watch the Discovery Channel because it shows a lot of interesting programs about amazing things and places in the world.

❻ Listen to each response and match it to the question it answers.

a. 1

b. 3

c. 2

❖ Extra Practice

Try answering one or more of these questions for extra practice. Use at least three sentences in your response to each question.

Sample Responses

1. How do you decide what to wear every day?

It is very difficult for me to decide what to wear every day. My friends and I love nice clothes. We try not to wear the same thing on the same day, so I usually take some outfits out of my closet and call my friends to make sure we are not planning to wear similar outfits. I can also get advice from them on what to wear.

2. What is your day like after lunch?

After lunch, I usually have three more classes at school. First, I have my advanced algebra class with Ms. Thompson. Then I have an English class, followed by a geography class.

3. Do you sometimes play games with your siblings or friends? What games do you play?

Yes, I sometimes play games with my older brother. We have a PlayStation, so we play lots of different games. My favorite games are sports games like soccer, though my brother prefers to solve puzzles.

4. If you had more time, what would you really like to do?

If I had more time, I would like to be able to relax more. Sometimes, I feel really exhausted towards the end of the week. I know my life is extremely busy, so I would like to have more time to just relax and think more about things.

Unit 10 Experiences

❶ **Listen to the speakers. Write the questions that they answer.**

a. Speaker #1: When was a time you <u>were</u> <u>really</u> <u>scared</u>?

b. Speaker #2: What is the best place <u>you</u> <u>have</u> <u>visited</u>?

c. Speaker #3: When do people <u>usually</u> <u>get</u> <u>nervous</u>?

❷ **Sort the words by writing them in the correct categories.**

Descriptions: hard, sad, exotic, high, happy, proud

Actions: feel, visit, remember, study, repeat, come

Things: letter, country, airport, university, culture, vacation

❹ **Choose one of the questions below. Prepare your answers to this question by writing notes below. Use the questions from part 3 to help with your notes.**

Answers will vary.

a. Describe a time when you felt really proud of yourself.

I felt really proud of myself when I got the letter with my TOEFL iBT score because it was a good score. I studied really hard for the test, and I didn't want to have to repeat it because it is a difficult test. I was both happy and relieved that I had done well on the test!

b. What day of your life do you think you would remember forever? Describe the experience.

I will always remember the day when I left my country to study abroad. That day, my whole family and all my friends came to the airport to say goodbye to me and wish me luck. I was happy that I had the opportunity to study abroad, but I was also sad to leave my family and friends.

c. Describe an experience you have had traveling to an exotic place.

When I was 14 years old, my family took me to Honolulu, Hawaii because we wanted to see this exotic place and to have our vacation there. The colors all around us looked so different, and the culture was very different from my own. The people were also very friendly.

❻ Listen to each response and match it to the question it answers.

a. 1

b. 3

c. 2

❖ **Extra Practice**

Try answering one or more of these questions for extra practice. Use at least three sentences in your response to each question.

Sample Responses

1. Describe an experience when you lied to somebody you love.

When I was 12, I did very poorly on some of my school tests. I didn't want to show my report card to my father, so I told him I didn't get one. When he asked the teacher about it, I got into big trouble.

2. Describe a time when you saw a sunrise or a sunset.

When I was 15 years old, I saw a really amazing sunrise. I think I will remember it forever. We were hiking in the Rocky Mountains, and one night we got up very early. My father woke me up to share that beautiful sunrise with him.

3. Describe a close relationship you have with someone. Why are you so close to this person?

I have a very close relationship with my best friend, Sarah, because I know we can trust each other. We became best friends after we both started school, and we have grown even closer since then.

4. Describe a time when you were very nervous.

I remember when I was at the hospital with my mom, and we were waiting for her blood test results. My mom had been sick for quite a while. She had heart problems, so that day we were at the hospital waiting for her doctor to tell us if she needed surgery. I was extremely nervous the whole day. Luckily, it was good news. She didn't need the operation after all!

Unit 11 **Family**

❶ Listen to the speakers. Write the questions that they answer.

a. **Speaker #1:** Where do <u>your</u> <u>grandparents</u> <u>live</u>?

b. **Speaker #2:** What are your <u>parents'</u> <u>jobs</u>?

c. **Speaker #3:** <u>How</u> <u>many</u> <u>children</u> does a typical family in your country have?

❷ Sort the words by writing them in the correct categories.

Descriptions: perfect, handsome, smart, strong, tall, responsible

Family Members: uncles, husband, grandparents, aunts, wife, siblings

Actions: annoy, celebrate, teach, get along, live, look up to

❹ Choose one of the questions below. Prepare your answers to this question by writing notes below. Use the questions from part 3 to help with your notes.

Answers will vary.

a. **Tell me about your favorite sister, brother, or cousin.**

My favorite brother's name is Ali. He is my older brother. I like him because he helps me and teaches me a lot of useful things. He is twenty years old. He is very tall and strong. Everyone thinks he is handsome. He is also smart and responsible, so I really look up to him.

b. **What is your idea of a perfect family?**

My idea of a perfect family is when parents, children, grandparents, uncles, aunts, and cousins all live close by so that they can help each other, spend time together, and celebrate together. Most of us live in the same city or close by. Some of my family members live about an hour's drive away. My uncle and his wife live in Italy, so we don't see them very much.

c. **Do you have any siblings or cousins? If so, how old are they? Do you get along well with them?**

Yes, I have two siblings and three cousins. My two older brothers are 15 and 17 years old, and my cousins are 7, 9, and 13. We all get along very well, though sometimes we get annoyed at my youngest cousin because he can get into things that he is not supposed to get into.

6 **Listen to each response and match it to the question it answers.**

a. 2

b. 1

c. 3

❖ **Extra Practice**

Try answering one or more of these questions for extra practice. Use at least three sentences in your response to each question.

Sample Responses

1. **Talk about your parents. What is the best thing about your mother or father?**

I love my parents very much because I would not have been able to achieve a lot of things in life without them. First, I would like to talk about my mom. She is extremely kind and generous. My dad is the wisest man I have ever known. He always gives me good advice about things.

2. **Who does the chores in your family? Who cleans, cooks, and does the laundry?**

We share the chores in my family because we all help our mother to keep the house clean. All the children are responsible for cleaning their own rooms. Our mom usually does the cooking because she is really good at it. My dad cleans the garage and takes care of the yard.

3. **Should parents give their children an allowance? How much should it be?**

Yes, I think parents should give their children an allowance because children sometimes need money for things. Also, children should have an

allowance so they can learn the value of money. I don't think it should be very much. Something like a few dollars should be enough because young kids don't need to buy a lot of things.

4. **Talk about one of your family traditions.**

It is our family tradition to celebrate New Year's Eve because we like spending special moments together as a family. We usually have a nice meal at home, and then we play some games together.

Unit 12 Feelings

1 **Listen to the speakers. Write the questions that they answer.**

a. **Speaker #1:** When do you <u>feel</u> <u>happy</u>?

b. **Speaker #2:** When do you <u>get</u> <u>annoyed</u>?

c. **Speaker #3:** When do you <u>bite</u> <u>your</u> <u>nails</u>?

2 **Sort the words by writing them in the correct categories.**

Things: notebook, quiz, grade, birdhouse, situation, project

Actions: participate, receive, change, present, catch, build

Descriptions: angry, ashamed, impatient, embarrassed, unfair, frustrated

4 **Choose one of the questions below. Prepare your answers to this question by writing notes below. Use the questions from part 3 to help with your notes.**

Answers will vary.

a. **What things make you feel frustrated and why? Describe a situation when you felt like that.**

I get really frustrated when I try hard to accomplish something but it does not come out the way I want. I feel like that because I tend to be very impatient. Once I tried to build a birdhouse, but I couldn't get it right, so I got very frustrated and gave up.

b. What things make you feel angry and why? Describe a situation when you felt like that.

I feel angry when something unfair happens, and I can't change it. I hate it when people are unfair to each other. For example, we were doing a group project at school, and one of the students was not participating enough. But after we presented the project well, we all received a good grade, including the student who didn't do much work.

c. What things make you feel embarrassed and why? Describe a situation when you felt like that.

I feel really embarrassed when I do something wrong and someone sees me do it. I feel like that because I know that what I am doing is wrong, and I feel ashamed when I am caught. For example, one day I was unprepared for a class quiz, so I decided to look in my notebook during the quiz. My teacher caught me doing it!

6 Listen to each response and match it to the question it answers.

a. **3**

b. **1**

c. **2**

❖ **Extra Practice**

Try answering one or more of these questions for extra practice. Use at least three sentences in your response to each question.

Sample Responses

1. What things make you feel tired and why? Describe a situation like that.

I feel really tired after I come back home from soccer practice. Because I try really hard to improve my skills, I practice a lot. When I get home all I want to do is go to bed, but I usually have lots of homework.

2. What things make you laugh and why? Describe a situation like that.

There are many things that make me laugh. I think I have a good sense of humor. I really enjoy funny movies, so I always go to see new comedies at the cinema. I enjoy funny novels, too, though not as much as movies.

3. What things make you cover your eyes and why? Describe a situation like that.

Scary things make me cover my eyes. I always do that when I watch something very scary because I try to separate myself from the scary scene. Once I was watching a horror movie with my friends, and it was really scary, so I covered my eyes every time something scary happened.

4. What things make you blush and why? Describe a situation like that.

When I feel embarrassed or find myself in an uncomfortable situation, I blush. I do that because I understand that I did or said something strange and other people saw or heard it. Once, my friends and I were at a party, and we were discussing this person that we didn't like very much. I was talking very loudly. Then, I turned around and I realized that person was right behind me. How embarrassing!

Unit 13 **Air Travel**

1 Listen to the speakers. Write the questions that they answer.

a. **Speaker #1:** Have you <u>flown</u> <u>on</u> <u>a plane</u>?

b. **Speaker #2:** What is the best way to <u>buy airline tickets</u>?

c. **Speaker #3:** What can people do <u>during flights</u>?

2 Sort the words by writing them in the correct categories.

Descriptions: large, domestic, convenient, early, major, international

Actions: make, fly, specify, provide, arrive, visit

Things: luggage, compartment, airplane, boarding pass, magazine, passport

④ Choose one of the questions below. Prepare your answers to this question by writing notes below. Use the questions from part 3 to help with your notes.

Answers will vary.

a. What airline companies are there in your country? Can you name some places where many people from your country go by plane?

There are three airlines in my country. One of them makes domestic flights. The other two provide international flights. People from my country fly to many other countries. For example, some people visit European countries, like France and Germany.

b. How many hours do you have to arrive at an airport before a flight? Explain.

You should arrive at the airport at least two hours before a flight because you need to have enough time to get your luggage checked in and go through immigration and security with your passport, boarding pass, and carry-on luggage. It's better to get to the airport early because all this can take up a lot of time.

c. Is carry-on luggage allowed on planes in your country? What items do you like to have with you on an airplane?

Yes, carry-on luggage is allowed on airplanes in my country, but it can't be very large because it has to fit in the overhead compartment or under the seat in front of you. Most airlines specify how big carry-on luggage can be, and people should follow these rules. I like to have my iPod, my laptop computer, and a book or a magazine to keep myself occupied on long flights.

⑥ Listen to each response and match it to the question it answers.

a. 3

b. 1

c. 2

❖ **Extra Practice**

Try answering one or more of these questions for extra practice. Use at least three sentences in your response to each question.

Sample Responses

1. On an airplane, would you prefer to sit by the window or by the aisle? Explain.

I prefer to sit by the window because I like to look out the window. I like to see the city, the roads, the cars, and the people, and I like to see how they get smaller and smaller as my plane takes off. Also, I like to look at the clouds.

2. Are you afraid of flying? Explain.

Yes, I am a little afraid of flying, though I have flown a lot. I have flown to other cities in my country and abroad, but every time I do, I keep thinking of the huge distance between my seat and the ground. I think take-off and landing are the scariest parts of a flight.

3. Describe the responsibilities of a flight attendant.

Flight attendants are supposed to make their passengers' traveling experience pleasant and to make sure everybody on their plane is safe. They need to make sure everyone is comfortable and has what they need. They also serve drinks and food during the flight.

4. After a flight, what do people do when they have arrived at their destination?

When people have arrived at their destination, they usually have to pass through immigration. They show their passport and get a stamp in it. Then they proceed to the baggage claim area to pick up their luggage.

Unit 14 Food

❶ Listen to the speakers. Write the questions that they answer.

a. **Speaker #1:** What is <u>your</u> <u>favorite</u> <u>food</u>?

b. Speaker #2: What is <u>the strangest</u> <u>food</u> you have tried?

c. Speaker #3: What does <u>the typical diet</u> in your country include?

❷ Sort the words by writing them in the correct categories.

Ingredients/Food: spices, spaghetti, rice, meatballs, waffles, lasagna

Things: instructions, television, dish, kitchen, recipes, cookbooks

Descriptions: fantastic, better, wonderful, awful, tasty, appetizing

❹ Choose one of the questions below. Prepare your answers to this question by writing notes below. Use the questions from part 3 to help with your notes

Answers will vary.

a. What type of food do you like to prepare? Why?

I like to prepare a traditional dish that we eat in my native country. It is called kielbasa. kielbasa is rice cooked with spiced lamb or chicken. Well, it's quite easy to prepare. It also tastes wonderful because of all of the different spices used in it.

b. Do you like to use recipes from cookbooks when preparing food? Explain.

No, I don't. I have tried to use recipes from cookbooks several times, but they just don't work for me, even though I use all the right ingredients and follow the instructions. Either the food doesn't taste good or it doesn't look appetizing. Once I tried to make lasagna, but it tasted awful. However, I can make very tasty spaghetti and meatballs!

c. Which of your parents is the better cook? What is your favorite food that he or she makes?

My mom is a better cook than my dad. As a matter of fact, I have never seen my dad in the kitchen cooking anything at all. My mom, however, is always there. She makes really delicious waffles for breakfast. They are fantastic!

❻ Listen to each response and match it to the question it answers.

a. 3

b. 1

c. 2

❖ Extra Practice

Try answering one or more of these questions for extra practice. Use at least three sentences in your response to each question.

Sample Responses

1. Who do you like to eat out with? Explain.

I like to eat out with my friends, of course, because we always have a lot of fun together when we go out. I can talk about things with them that I wouldn't talk to my parents about.

2. Do you think it is better to take friends to a restaurant or to a movie? Explain.

I think it is better to take friends to a restaurant because you get a chance to talk and listen to them. You can have a good conversation over some good food and hear about the new things that have happened in your friends' lives. At a movie, you don't get a chance to talk.

3. Is going on a diet good for a person's health? Explain.

Going on a diet can be beneficial for some overweight people because they get a chance to lose some weight and to improve their health. Eating healthy food and doing regular exercise makes people feel better mentally, too.

4. What special foods do people prepare for celebrations and holidays in your country?

There are special foods that we prepare to celebrate special occasions in my culture. They come from traditional Mexican foods and the traditional style of eating. For example, we prepare tamales, posole, burritos, and mole. Tamales are little bundles of filling wrapped in corn leaves. I love them!

Unit 15 Fruits and Vegetables

1 Listen to the speakers. Write the questions that they answer.

  a. Speaker #1: What are <u>your</u> <u>favorite</u> <u>vegetables</u>?

  b. Speaker #2: Have you ever <u>tried</u> <u>to</u> <u>grow</u> fruits or vegetables?

  c. Speaker #3: What is <u>the</u> <u>difference</u> <u>between</u> fruits and vegetables?

2 Sort the words by writing them in the correct categories.

  Fruits: limes, oranges, pineapples, bananas, lemons, apples

  Vegetables: onions, carrots, beets, cabbage, broccoli, potatoes

  Descriptions: favorite, poisonous, tangy, fresh, sweet, dangerous

4 Choose one of the questions below. Prepare your answers to this question by writing notes below. Use the questions from part 3 to help with your notes

  Answers will vary.

  a. What fruits do people grow in your native country? Name one of your favorite desserts made with fruit. Describe this dessert.

  Many farmers in my country usually grow fruits like bananas and pineapples. I guess citrus fruits are popular in my country. In some places in my country, you can see orange, lemon, and lime trees. My favorite dessert is orange ice cream, which is usually made with fresh oranges, sugar, and milk. It is both sweet and tangy at the same time.

  b. What vegetables does your mother or grandmother use to prepare soup? How does she prepare it?

  My grandma can make really delicious vegetable soup. She uses fresh cabbage, broccoli, onions, carrots, beets, potatoes, and spices. To prepare it,

she puts all these ingredients in a pot and leaves it on the stove to cook overnight.

  c. Do you think it makes a difference if fruits and vegetables are grown with chemical fertilizers and pesticides? Explain.

  Yes, it does make a difference because I think now we know a lot more about how chemicals can affect our health. There has been a lot of research in this area. Using pesticides keeps insects away from fruits and vegetables, but they can be dangerous to our health because pesticides are poisonous. When I buy fruits and vegetables, it is important for me to know where they came from and whether or not chemicals were used to grow them.

6 Listen to each response and match it to the question it answers.

  a. 3

  b. 1

  c. 2

❖ **Extra Practice**

  Try answering one or more of these questions for extra practice. Use at least three sentences in your response to each question.

  Sample Responses

  1. Why is it important to eat fruits and vegetables? How many should you eat each day?

  Fruits and vegetables are very important for our health because they provide our bodies with all the necessary vitamins and minerals that we need. We should try to eat four to five servings of fruits and vegetables a day.

  2. What is your favorite fruit? Why? What dish can you prepare with your favorite fruit? How do you prepare it?

  My favorite fruit is the apple because it is very sweet and also very good for our teeth. I can prepare an apple pie from apples. To do this, you need a couple of apples, some sugar, and a pie shell. It's easy to make.

3. What does the saying "One rotten apple spoils the whole barrel" mean? Do you have a saying with a similar meaning in your culture?

This means that if there is one bad or negative thing, such as an apple or even a person, it can spoil all the positive things around it. Yes, there is a proverb with a similar meaning in my culture, which is "Don't put a moldy potato in your potato basket."

4. What does it mean when someone is comparing apples to oranges? Explain. Do you have a similar saying in your culture?

People use this phrase when they want to emphasize that they are talking about two completely different things because apples and oranges are very different. For example, it would be difficult to say whether a coat was nicer than a meal because these are two very different things. There is a similar saying in my culture. In fact, if you translate this into my native language, the saying is exactly the same.

Unit 16 Giving Directions

❶ Listen to the speakers. Write the questions that they answer.

a. Speaker #1: What is the easiest way to get to your house from school?

b. Speaker #2: Where is the nearest post office?

c. Speaker #3: Where is a good book store?

❷ Sort the words by writing them in the correct categories.

Places/Things: grocery store, intersection, bus stop, traffic light, hospital, market

Descriptions: first, far, left, straight, nearest, right

Actions: turn, give directions, walk, set up, see, get off

❹ Choose one of the questions below. Prepare your answers to this question by writing notes below. Use the questions from part 3 to help with your notes.

Answers will vary.

a. You want your friend to visit one of your relatives with you. Give him directions from your home to your relative's home.

My Aunt Cecile's house is not far from my house, so you can walk there. First, go straight down Main Street and turn right onto Willow Drive. Walk two blocks until you get to the traffic light and turn left. Her house is number four. The front door is painted green.

b. You need some fruit and your friend offers to help you. Give him directions from your house to the nearest grocery store.

The nearest grocery store is quite far, so we will have to drive there. Go down Main Street and turn right onto Rosewood Road. Drive to the traffic lights at the intersection of Grant and Stone Street. Turn left onto Stone Street and you will see the grocery store.

c. Your aunt is visiting from another city. You suggest she visit your local farmer's market on the weekend. Give her directions from your home to the market.

Our local farmers set up their market on Woodrow Street every weekend. To get there, you should take bus number two to Stanford Road. Get off at the first bus stop in front of the hospital, and walk two or three blocks along Stanford Road. You will see the market right next to the gas station on Stanford.

❻ Listen to each response and match it to the question it answers.

a. 1

b. 3

c. 2

❖ Extra Practice

Try answering one or more of these questions for extra practice. Use at least three sentences in your response to each question.

Sample Responses

1. **Describe how to get from your house to school.**

   The school is not far from my house, so you can walk. First, you go down Oak Road and turn left onto Maple Avenue. Then, at the intersection of Maple and Birch, turn right. That's it.

2. **Give directions to the nearest supermarket from your house.**

   The nearest supermarket is downtown, so you will have to take bus number 5 to get there. Get off at Maple Avenue and then turn left at Sinclair Road. The supermarket is on your right.

3. **What is the fastest way to get downtown from your house?**

   The fastest way to get from my house to downtown is by subway. The subway station is just around the corner. Take the blue line north, and get off at the City Hall station. That station is in the middle of downtown.

4. **Recommend a good place to get a haircut. Describe how to get there.**

   My hair stylist works at Kim's Beauty Salon on Broadway Avenue. First, drive to the intersection of Main and Stone and take a left. Then, drive for about one minute and you will see it on the left.

Unit 17 Health

❶ **Listen to the speakers. Write the questions that they answer.**

   a. **Speaker #1:** What is one thing you learned <u>in physical education class</u>?

   b. **Speaker #2:** What <u>over</u>-<u>the</u>-<u>counter medication</u> do you take?

   c. **Speaker #3:** How often do you <u>go to the gym</u>?

❷ **Sort the words by writing them in the correct categories.**

   Descriptions: healthy, exhausted, important, miserable, simple, tired

   Actions: repair, restore, help, feel, injure, sneeze

Things: bodies, allergy, vitamins, tasks, air, pollen

❹ **Choose one of the questions below. Prepare your answers to this question by writing notes below. Use the questions from part 3 to help with your notes.**

Answers will vary.

   a. **Why is it important to get enough sleep? What are some negative effects of not getting enough sleep? How much sleep should you get each night?**

   Sleep is a vital part of our lives because our bodies need sleep to restore ourselves after each day. When we do not get enough sleep, we get exhausted easily, and even simple tasks can seem difficult.

   b. **Why is it important to get enough vitamins? Explain.**

   Getting enough vitamins is very important for our bodies because they need vitamins to be healthy. Without vitamins, our bodies can't function normally. For example, vitamins can help the body repair itself when a part of it gets injured.

   c. **Do you or any of your friends have allergies? Describe some negative effects of having allergies.**

   Yes, I have a friend who is allergic to pollen. Because of her allergy, she can't do activities outside when there is a lot of pollen in the air. For example, in the spring, she sneezes a lot and her eyes always water. Her nose gets very red, and she feels tired and miserable.

❻ **Listen to each response and match it to the question it answers.**

   a. **2**

   b. **3**

   c. **1**

❖ **Extra Practice**

Try answering one or more of these questions for extra practice. Use at least three sentences in your response to each question.

Sample Responses

1. Have you ever had a massage? Would you like to have one/another one? Why?

Yes, I once went to a spa to have a massage and a body wrap for my skin. It was very relaxing. The masseuse took time to massage my back and my arms. I would like to have another one sometime because it really relaxed me and made me feel great.

2. Give reasons why physical education (PE) classes are important.

PE classes are very important at school because they give schoolchildren a chance to exercise during the day. As we know, students spend a lot of time sitting at their desks, so getting some exercise during the day is very important. It keeps their muscles strong and their circulation systems working well.

3. Why is it important to take care of your teeth?

It is important to take care of our teeth because we have only one set of adult teeth in our lives. We have to make sure they stay strong and healthy and serve us for a long time. If all your teeth fall out, you can only eat liquids, like soup or smoothies.

4. Give examples of bad habits that negatively influence people's health. Explain.

Bad habits that negatively influence our health are smoking, consuming alcohol, using drugs, and having sedentary lifestyles. These can all contribute to bad health. In fact, these kinds of habits can kill you!

Unit 18   **The Internet**

❶ Listen to the speakers. Write the questions that they answer.

a. Speaker #1: Why do people like to <u>use the Internet</u>?

b. Speaker #2: What can happen if you <u>spend too much time</u> online?

c. Speaker #3: Should <u>schools allow students</u> to use the Internet?

❷ Sort the words by writing them in the correct categories.

Internet Vocabulary: file, download, website, program, access, post

Where People Use the Internet: at school, at home, in a library, coffee shops, Internet café, at work

Why People Use the Internet: send pictures, buy things, research, meet people, send email, sell things

❹ Choose one of the questions below. Prepare your answers to this question by writing notes below. Use the questions from part 3 to help with your notes.

Answers will vary.

a. Why is it convenient to have and use email?

It is very convenient to have and use email because it is another fast and easy way to contact somebody besides using a telephone. All you need is an email program on your computer. Secondly, email is free, so you don't need to pay anything. I really enjoy communicating with people from around the world.

b. What are the advantages of having Internet access at home?

There are many advantages of having Internet access at home. First, you can go online anytime if you have a computer in your house. You don't have to go to the library or your school. I like to go on the Internet and check my email in the evenings or sometimes in the morning before I go to school.

c. Describe how people use the Internet.

People use the Internet for various reasons. Some of them use it for business to communicate with their business partners in other countries, to send emails, business letters, and orders. Some people use it for personal reasons, like playing games or shopping. I have never bought anything online. My dad has bought many things online, and he has also sold lots of things for his home business.

6 **Listen to each response and match it to the question it answers.**

a. 1

b. 3

c. 2

❖ **Extra Practice**

Try answering one or more of these questions for extra practice. Use at least three sentences in your response to each question.

Sample Responses

1. **How can the Internet be improved? Provide specific examples.**

    The Internet can be improved if we improve its reliability. Now, many of the things that are on the Internet are untrue. It makes it difficult for us to trust things that we read.

2. **How does the Internet help people do business all over the world?**

    The Internet helps people do business in many ways. The Internet never closes, so businesses and customers have access to products at all times. The Internet also lets us buy things from people very easily from all corners of the world.

3. **Do you think the Internet can be addictive? Explain.**

    Yes I think the Internet can be addictive just like TV. If people constantly look at things and are constantly entertained by something, they might start to feel dependent on that thing to feel good. Like anything that we enjoy, the Internet can be addictive and should be used moderately.

4. **What information about yourself should you never provide online? Why?**

Identity theft has become a huge problem due to the Internet. People should never give out personal identification numbers over the Internet. They should also closely guard their bank account information. If the wrong people get the information, they can ruin someone's life.

Unit 19 **Jobs and Occupations**

1 **Listen to the speakers. Write the questions that they answer.**

a. **Speaker #1:** What job would you never want to have?

b. **Speaker #2:** What kind of jobs have you had?

c. **Speaker #3:** What is an interesting job that one of your relatives has?

2 **Sort the words by writing them in the correct categories.**

People/Things: career, future, politician, position, president, responsibilities

Actions: accept, get a job, occupy, require, take care of, travel

Descriptions: common, married, satisfied, single, successful, traditional

4 **Choose one of the questions below. Prepare your answers to this question by writing notes below. Use the questions from part 3 to help with your notes.**

Answers will vary.

a. **What are typical jobs for men in your country?**

    Men in my country occupy various positions. Common jobs for men are a police officer, businessman, doctor, fire fighter, or politician. Actually, no woman has ever run for president. I really believe that a woman could do a great job as president.

b. **What is more important for women in your country: to have a career or to take care of their families?**

Traditionally, it is more important for women in my country to take care of their families than to have a career. My family didn't really follow this tradition. My parents wanted all of their children to work in a successful career. Hopefully I can have both a successful career and a successful family life, but it is hard to say what will happen in the future.

c. Would you accept a job that required a lot of traveling? Explain.

Yes, I would accept a job that required a lot of traveling, as long as I was not married. After I got married, I would choose to spend more time with my wife and my children. As a single person, I would not have the responsibilities of supporting a family, so I could do more things that I wanted to.

6 Listen to each response and match it to the question it answers.

a. 1

b. 3

c. 2

❖ Extra Practice

Try answering one or more of these questions for extra practice. Use at least three sentences in your response to each question.

Sample Responses

1. If you had a choice, what would you choose to become? Why?

If I had a choice, I would like to become an elementary school teacher. Elementary school teachers are very important because they help to shape kids' attitudes and outlook on life. Because I could do so much to help kids get started on the right track, I want to be an elementary school teacher.

2. How do companies in your country reward workers/employees?

Companies can reward workers in my country in many different ways. First, workers can receive

bonuses in the form of money or extra days off. Companies often take out their entire staff to a really fancy restaurant. The really large companies have retreats at mountain or beach resorts to allow their staff time to relax and bond together as a team.

3. Where and how do you find a good job?

I think there are many ways that you can find a good job. One way is to establish a network of friends who are already successful at their jobs, so they might recommend you. Another way is to search through a newspaper's classified ads. If I knew the company I wanted to work for, I would go to its website and apply directly for a job with the company.

4. What is a workaholic?

Workaholics are people who care only about their jobs and disregard the rest of their lives. They are always the first ones to come to work and the last ones to leave. They rarely have hobbies or other interests outside of work.

Unit 20 Literature and Books

❶ Listen to the speakers. Write the questions that they answer.

a. **Speaker #1:** How often do you <u>read</u> <u>for</u> <u>fun</u>?

b. **Speaker #2:** Have you read a book that is <u>also</u> <u>a</u> <u>movie</u>?

c. **Speaker #3:** Why is it important to <u>read</u> <u>classical</u> <u>literature</u>?

❷ Sort the words by writing them in the correct categories.

Things to Read: newspapers, labels, posters, comic books, street signs, bus schedules

In a Book: characters, plot, settings, illustrations, pictures, events

Places to Study: library, park, living room, school, bedroom, computer room

4 **Choose one of the questions below. Prepare your answers to this question by writing notes below. Use the questions from part 3 to help with your notes.**

Answers will vary.

a. Give examples of everyday activities that require good reading skills.

There are many activities in our everyday lives that require good reading skills. For example, we read newspapers to learn the news. We read labels on boxes, cans, and jars to know what we are eating. We need to read street signs so we don't get lost. Reading is important if we want to learn something new.

b. Is it important to have pictures, maps, and illustrations in books? Why?

Yes, it is. Pictures, maps, and illustrations give us a visual image of the main characters, events, and settings of books. Also, pictures help us understand the story. Sometimes there are too many pictures, though. I still think the best part of reading a book is imagining things in the story. A lot of my school books have pictures, but that's because we need pictures to help us learn more about science and other subjects.

c. Why do some people prefer to study in the library?

Some people prefer to study in the library because they can do research, or they can find more books on the subject that they are studying. Also, the atmosphere in the library is good for helping you focus on what you're studying. I usually study in my room at home. The library is too quiet. If I study there, I usually fall asleep.

6 **Listen to each response and match it to the question it answers.**

a. 2

b. 3

c. 1

❖ **Extra Practice**

Try answering one or more of these questions for extra practice. Use at least three sentences in your response to each question.

Sample Responses

1. What is the last book that you read? Describe the plot.

The last book that I read was a piece of non-fiction called *Adventure Capitalist*. The man in the book is a retired millionaire from New York who spends three years driving around the world with his wife. He drives across all the continents. The book is a travel diary of his experiences and observations of what he saw during his journey.

2. Do you like reading classical literature? Why or why not?

Yes, I do. I love reading classical literature because it's a perfect way to learn about the history of a country. It also exposes me to new vocabulary and sayings that are no longer used. My favorite classical writer is Geoffrey Chaucer. He wrote *The Canterbury Tales*. It is a remarkable book because it is so funny, despite being written almost 800 years ago.

3. What is one of the most famous books in your country? What is it about?

One of the most famous books in my country is called *The Adventures of Tom Sawyer*. *Tom Sawyer* was written by Mark Twain and is about a boy who grew up in America in the 1800s. The boy is very mischievous and always seems to be getting in and out of trouble. The story talks about life while growing up in a small town in America.

4. Do you think books will be important in the future or will the Internet replace them? Explain.

I think books will be as important in the future as the Internet. Nothing can replace the value of an ancient book or a manuscript that can teach us about history and writing styles. I also think that there is still a connection between a person and a book that will never be replaced. Because of this, books will never be replaced.